NEW AND COLLECTED POEMS
1964–2006

Also by Ishmael Reed

Collected Works
The Reed Reader

Novels
The Free Lance Pallbearers
Yellow-Back Radio Broke-Down
Mumbo Jumbo
The Last Days of Louisiana Red
Flight To Canada
Reckless Eyeballing
The Terrible Twos
The Terrible Threes
Japanese By Spring

Poetry
Conjure: Selected Poems, 1963-1970
Chattanooga
A Secretary to the Spirits
New & Collected Poems

Essays and Nonfiction
Blues City, A Walk in Oakland
Another Day at the Front, Dispatches from the Race War
Airing Dirty Laundry
Writin' Is Fightin'
God Made Alaska For The Indians
Shrovetide In Old New Orleans

Anthology Editor
*From Totems to Hip-Hop: A Multicultural Anthology
of Poetry Across the Americas, 1900-2001*
and others

Plays
Tough Love
C Above C Above High C
The Preacher and the Rapper
Hubba City
Savage Wilds
Mother Hubbard

NEW AND COLLECTED POEMS

POEMS   1964–2006

Ishmael Reed

CARROLL & GRAF PUBLISHERS
NEW YORK

NEW AND COLLECTED POEMS, 1964–2006

Carroll & Graf Publishers
An Imprint of Avalon Publishing Group, Inc.
245 West 17th Street
11th Floor
New York, NY 10011

AVALON
publishing group incorporated

Library of Congress Cataloging-in-Publication Data is available.

ISBN-10: 0-78671-788-2
ISBN-13: 978-0-78671-788-0

9 8 7 6 5 4 3 2 1

Printed in the United States of America
Distributed by Publishers Group West

Dedicated to Carla

I Don't Want to Set the World on
Fire; I Just Want to Start a Flame
in Your Heart

–Horace Heidt

CONTENTS

CHATTANOOGA

A SECRETARY TO THE SPIRITS

POINTS OF VIEW

NEW VERSE, 1989–2006

INTRODUCTION

I was in seventh grade when my mother commissioned me to write a poem, celebrating the birthdate of a fellow employee. I don't remember the contents, only that it rhymed. This was 1950, and it was my first "occasional poem." (Throughout my career as a poet, I have continued to write occasional poems. "Epistolary Monologue," for example, was commissioned by a group of Irish-American intellectuals who had organized a protest against a dinner for Queen Elizabeth that was hosted by Ronald and Nancy Reagan at San Francisco's De Young Museum, and Jerry Brown, the Mayor of Oakland, commissioned me to write his inaugural poem. Both poems appear in this collection.)

Influenced by Nathaniel West, I wrote fiction at the University of Buffalo and, in 1957, took poetry classes. It was at Buffalo that I was introduced to Yeats, Auden, and Pound, whose influence can be seen in the poem "The Ghost of Birmingham" (printed in *The Liberator* magazine in the mid-sixties and illustrated by the late Tom Feelings). I was especially taken by Auden, who was later my next-door neighbor when I lived in a brownstone on Saint Mark's Place in New York. Unlike some other modernists, Auden was clear, spare, and crisp in his language.

In 1963, I joined the Umbra workshop, a literary boot camp. We were very hard on each other; some would say cruel. But it was through this workshop that I rid my writing of its affectations. It was also through the Umbra workship that I met Langston Hughes, who was responsible for my first novel being published by Doubleday.

I have been fortunate to receive support from great writers. In the mid-sixties, I was published in Walter Lowenfel's *Poets of Today* and Langston Hughes's *Poetry of the Negro*. I also received very helpful advice about my work from poet Gloria Oden. And when my work took a hammering from the cultural revolution of the moment, during the eighties, Gwendolyn Brooks awarded me a prize, named for the late critic, George Kent. Irish writers have influenced black writers since at least the 1930s: The exploration of Celtic mythology by Yeats and his circle led me to use Egyptian allusions in my early poetry as a way of avoiding colonial influences. Toward the end of the sixties, a painting by Joe Overstreet that included ververs, the geometric designs or landing patterns for loas or "saints," led me to study African religion in New Orleans and Haiti. The Irish writers had, for me, inspired a way to resist a model imposed from the outside. This was to return to one's roots. For them it was the Celtic Revival. For me Neo-Hoo Dooism "Hoo Doo" stories—which used magical realism before there was a term for it—had been part of the oral tradition and recorded by writers like Charles Chesnutt, Zora Neale Hurston, and Langston Hughes. In the late sixties, Steve Cannon, Quincy Troupe, Curtis Lyle, and I made a literary pilgrimage to New Orleans, where we assembled around the grave site of Marie Laveau, HooDoo Queen and healer, the Widow Paris (the name inscribed on her tomb she was married to a man named Paris). I called my work Neo-Hoo Dooism, as a way of recalling this past literary and oral history. This move baffled some critics and one of them even called my work "arcane." Neither he nor I knew at the time that African religion had millions of followers in the Caribbean and South America. In Brazil, its power rivals that of the Catholic Church and with the migration of people from the Caribbean and South and Central America, African religion is becoming the fastest-growing religion in the United States.

My research into African religion began with a reading of Roger Tallant's primitive nonfiction work *VooDoo in New Orleans* and continues with my study of the Yoruba language. Since most African captives originated in Western Nigeria, it is not surprising that many entities associated with the Yoruba pantheon would carry over into our hemisphere, with Sango, Ogun, and Oshun and Oya, the Nigerian equivalent to Catholic saints. Sango, associated with war, and Oshun and Oya, daughters of the god Olodumare, are among the most popular in this hemisphere, although there are hundreds of others. New ones arise all of the time.

This collection ends with my translation of an excerpt from Fungawa's *Igbo Olodumare* (*The Forest of God*), which I have entitled "Snake War." I was assisted in this translation by my teacher for over a decade, Ade Amoloran, who is not responsible for the liberties that I've taken with this text.

We all suffer because our political leaders—and the cultural leaders who tutor them at places like Harvard and Yale—have a cramped view of the world, in which something they refer to as "The West" towers above all civilizations past and present. This is the attitude that drove

President Lyndon Johnson to ignore Jack Valenti's advice to study the history and culture of Indo-China and accounts for the ignorant pronouncements of the cable networks' Islam experts, whose observations are ridiculed by Muslim intellectuals. This disrespect for the cultures of others leads to generations of African American youngsters who haven't a clue about African or African American cultures. The late Stanley "Tookie" Williams, co-founder of The Crips, a dangerous gang that did much to set back the gains African Americans made during the sixties and seventies and who was executed by the State of California, said that his career might have been different if he'd had a father with some knowledge of African American history and culture.

Like Malcolm X before him, the prison library was more helpful to him than the missionary educational system that denies African American culture.

In Japan and Nigeria, when you make an attempt to write in their languages, people appreciate it so much that they invite you to dinner and give you gifts. The habit among Eurocentric writers and scholars of dismissing African religion (think of such terms as "voodoo economics," or "voodoo scholarship") is unfortunate because it discourages many of those who depend upon them for cultural direction from learning about a source that has produced great painting music, writing, and dance. Despite the attempt to denigrate African religion, or even eliminate it from the cultural mix, many followers of African religion are members of races other than black. As one Brazilian Temple Mother said, "All roads lead to God." That idea suits me and it shows the essential genius of African religion: its strength is that it draws from disparate influences. On some altars you might find assemblages that include Hindu, Christian, and African cultures in addition to items associated with popular culture. I consider myself to be a Universalist. In fact, most of the poems printed in this collection are of a secular nature. "Gethsemane Park," a libretto that I wrote, and hired the great composer Carmen Moore to set to music, gives a Yoruba interpretation of books in the New Testament. In this version, Jesus of Nazareth is not a deity, but a saint. He never appears but possesses "the least of those among humanity," that is, the poor and the downtrodden. When Judas is asked by Beelzebub to identify Jesus with a kiss, Judas kisses all of the poor who are assembled because they collectively represent the spirit of Jesus. For me Jesus of Nazareth is no deity. In my libretto's scheme, he becomes a sort of patron saint of the homeless, the sick, and the frail. He is an Orisha, that is, an "invisible," taking over the bodies of others. Some critics were offended because a physical Jesus never appeared on stage. Lacking an understanding of African religion, they were awaiting the arrival on stage of somebody like Charlton Heston. The key lesson that I do take from Yoruba religion is from the parable in which a traveler finds himself in a strange country, away from his gods, and the only god that he can depend upon is his own mind.

 This collection includes four previous books: *Conjure, Chattanooga, A Secretary to the Spirits,* and *Points of View,* as well as *New Verse, 1989-2006* and, finally, *Gethsemane Park.*

Conjure, which includes poems written from the early sixties to 1970 and was published in 1972, finds me searching for an aesthetic other than the ones that had been presented to me during my Western-rooted education.

Chattanooga (1974) continues these experiments with nods to American history and folklore. The poem "A Secretary to the Spirits," a volume published by Nok, a Nigerian publishing company, ends the quest for an aesthetic home. It was during this period that I felt comfortable with a style that had been created from multiple influences.

Points of View was written during a period of intense woodshedding, that is, an intense period of isolation and reflection. Something like Sonny Rollins's *Bridge* period. Some of the poems were written in Sitka, Alaska, where I lived in the home of Alfred Perkins one summer, chief of the Tlingit Frog Klan and a man endowed with the ability to read mountains. It was during this trip that I discovered that totem poles were actually "books" of literature.

Gethsemane Park was begun in 1989. The first poem in this section of the book was based upon a newspaper photo of the former Soviet foreign minister Andrei Gromyko shown seated alone on a park bench while the Soviet Empire was beginning to dissolve.

In the 1980s my poetry took a turn as a result of a producer, Kip Hanrahan, having invited a number of leading jazz composers to set some of my poetry and songs to music. I walked into The Soul Brother's Kitchen on Telegraph Avenue one day to buy my weekly gumbo, and they were playing "Betty's Ball Blues," a song of mine that Taj Mahal set to music. The customers seemed to be enjoying it. At that point I decided to write more songs. Kip has produced three Conjure CDs, and I have toured with the Conjure band since 1993. Among the highlights of my career as a poet were when a gathering of Nigerian scholars and writers responded favorably to a song that I wrote in Yoruba in 1999 ("Azabu Kissaten De, At a Café in Azabu" and "Mo Jinde Loni, I Died Yesterday" are printed here) and when a song I wrote in Japanese received an enthusiastic response from an audience at the Blue Note in Tokyo in 2003. My songs and poetry have been performed and recorded by Little Jimmy Scott, Bobby Womack, Mary Wilson of the Supremes, Eddie Harris, Olu Dara, Robert Jason, Cream's Jack Bruce, and others.

There are probably more poets writing now than ever before in American history. Good poetry can come from writers of different backgrounds and different regions of the country. It is perhaps the most democratic of all writing forms. I have been fortunate enough to have mine printed and even sung.

—Ishmael Reed
Oakland, California
February 2, 2006

NEW AND COLLECTED POEMS
1964–2006

CONJURE

The Ghost in Birmingham

The only Holy Ghost in Birmingham is Denmark Vesey's Holy Ghost, brooding, moving in and out of things. No one notices the figure in antique cloak of the last century, haunting the pool games, talking of the weather with a passerby, attending mass meetings, standing guard, coming up behind each wave of protest, reloading a pistol. No one notices the antique figure in shabby clothing, moving in and out of things—rallies of moonshine gatherings—who usurps a pulpit and preaches a fire sermon, plucking the plumage of a furious hawk, a sparrow having passively died, moving in and out of chicken markets, watching sparrow habits become hawk habits, through bar stools and greenless parks, beauty salons, floating games, going somewhere, haranguing the crowds, his sleeves rolled up like a steelworker's, hurling epithets at the pharoah's club-wielding brigade, under orders to hunt down the firstborn of each low lit hearth.

There are no bulls in America in the sense of great symbols, which preside over resuscitation of godheads, that shake the dead land green. Only the "bull" of Birmingham, papier mâché, ten dollars down monthly terms, carbon copy mock heroic American variety of bullhood, who told a crowded room of flashbulbs that there was an outsider moving in and out of things that night, a spectre who flashed through the night like Pentecost.

He's right, there was.

Not the spook of the Judaic mystery, the universal immersed in the particular. Not the outsider from unpopular mysteries, a monstrous dialectic waddling through the corridors of his brain, but the nebulous presence hidden by flashbulbing events in Birmingham, Metempsychosis stroking the air.

Pragma the bitch has a knight errant called Abbadon, in the old texts the advocate of dreadful policies. The whore, her abominations spilling over, her stinking afterbirths sliming their way towards a bay of pigs, has a bland and well-groomed knight errant who said that "if we hand down a few more decisions, pile up paper, snap a few more pictures by Bachrach of famous people before grand rhetorical columns of the doric order, perhaps they will stop coming out into the streets in Raleigh, Greensboro, Jackson and Atlanta (sometimes called the Athens of the south).

Pragma's well-groomed and bland procurer is on long
    distance manufacturing heroes,
Heroes who bray in sirens screaming in from Idlewild,
    winging in from points south,
Their utterances cast into bronze by press-card-carrying
    harpies, those creatures of distorted reality.

O ebony-limbed Osiris, what clown folk singer or acrobat
    shall I place the tin wreath upon?
When will Osiris be scattered over 100 ghettos?

Heroes are ferried in by motorcycle escorts, their faces cast
    into by Pointillism, by Artzybasheff,
Sculptor of Henry Luce's America.

Introducing the King of Birmingham, sometimes called the
    anointed one,
Who receives the tin wreath across Americana banquet
    rooms,
His hands dripping with blood like a fanatical monk as
    rebellion squirms on the stake.

Introducing the Black Caligula, who performs a strip tease
    of the psyche,
Between Tiffany ads and Vat 69, giving up a little pussy for
    a well-groomed and bland knight errant.

O ebony-limbed Osiris, what knight club tap dancing char-
    latan shall I place the tin wreath upon?
All things are flowing said the poet when gods ambushed
    gods:
        Khan follows Confucius
        Light follows darkness
Tin wreathed heroes are followed by the figure in antique
    clothes, obscured by the flashbulbing events in Birmingham.
Metempsychosis in the air.

The Jackal-Headed Cowboy

We were—clinging to our arboreal—rustled
by a poplin dude so fast that even now
we mistake big mack trucks flying
confederate crossbones for rampaging
steer, leaping into their sandpaper hides
and lassoing their stubble faced drivers as they roar into
corn flaked greasy spoons.

We span the spic and spanned cesspools
nerves rankling like hot headed guerrillas
bayoneting artery routes and crawling through
our bowels with blades in their teeth.

Our mohair suits, our watches, our horn
rimmed glasses and several telephones
petition us to slow down as we forget
whose soupcan we swim.

We stand at Brooklyn Bridge like
mayakovsky before, deafened by the nuts
and bolts and clogged in the comings and
goings of goings of Usura

We are homesick weary travelers in the

Jungian sense and miss the brew of the
long night's pipe.

Our dreams point like bushy mavericks to
hawking game and scattering ripple falls.
We will swing from giant cables as if
they were hemp, hacking away at sky
scrapers till they tumble into christmas crowds.

We will raid chock full O nuts untying
apron strings crouching stealthily in the streets
breaking up conference rooms sweeping away
forms memo pads, ransoming bank presidents
shoving dollar bills through their mahogany jaws.

We will sit on Empire Sofas listening to
Gabrieli's fortissimo trumpets blare for
stewed and staggering Popes as Tom Tom mallets
beat the base of our brains.
We will leap tall couplets in a single bound
and chant chant Chant until our pudgy swollen
lips go on strike.
Our daughters will shake rattle roll and slop
snapping their fingers until grandfather
clocks' knees buckle and Tudor mansions free
their cobwebs.

Our mothers will sing shout swing and foam
making gothic spires get happy clapping the
night like blown up Zeppelin.

We will sizzle burn crackle and fry like combs
snapping the naps of Henri Christophe's daughters.
and We will scramble breasts bleating like
some tribe run amuck up and down desecrating
cosmotological graveyard factories.
and We will mash stock exchange bugs till
their sticky brown insides spill out like
reams of ticker tape.
and We will drag off yelling pinching bawling
shouting pep pills, detergents, acne powders,
clean rooms untampered maiden heads finger bowls
napkins renaissance glassware time subscriptions
reducing formulas
—please call before visiting—
—very happy to make your acquaintanceship i'm sure—
and boil down one big vat of unanimal stew
topped with kegs and kegs of whipped dynamite
and cheery smithereens.
and then We will rush like crazed antelopes
with our bastard babies number books mojo goofer
dusting razor blades chicken thighs spooky ha'nts
daddygracing fatherdivining jack legged preaching

bojangles sugar raying mamas into one scorching
burning lake and have a jigging hoedown with the
Quadrilling Sun.
and the panting moneygrabbing landlord
leeching redneck judges will scuffle
the embankment and drag the lipstick sky outside.
and their fuzzy patriarchs from Katzenjammer orphic
will offer hogmaws and the thunder bird and their overseers
will offer elixir bottles of pre punch cards
and the protocol hollering thunder will announce
our main man who'll bathe us and swathe us.
and Our man's spur jingles'll cause the clouds to
kick the dust in flight.
And his gutbucketing rompity bump will
cause sweaty limp flags to furl retreat
and the Jackal-headed cowboy will ride reins
whiplashing his brass legs and knobby hips.
And fast draw Anubis with his crank letters from Ra
will Gallop Gallop Gallop

our mummified profiled trail boss
as our swashbuckling storm fucking mob rides shot
gun for the moon and the whole sieged stage coach
of the world will heave and rock as we
bang stomp shuffle stampede cartwheel and cakewalk our
way into Limbo.

The Gangster's Death

how did he die/ O if i told you,
you would slap your hand
                         against your forehead
and say good grief/ if I gripped you
by the lapel and told how they dumped
   thalidomide hand grenades
into his blood stream and/
                       how they injected
a cyst into his spirit the size of an egg
which grew and grew until floating
   gangrene encircled the globe
and/ how guerrillas dropped from trees like
mean pythons
   and squeezed out his life
so that jungle birds fled their perches/
so that hand clapping monkeys   tumbled
   from branches and/
how twelve year olds snatched B-52's
   from the skies with their bare hands and/
how betty grable couldn't open a hershey bar
   without the wrapper exploding and/
how thin bent women wrapped bicycle chains
   around their knuckles saying
   we will fight until the last bra or/
   give us bread or shoot us/ and/

how killing him became childs play
in Danang in Mekong in Santo Domingo

   and how rigor mortis was sprinkled
in boston soups
   giving rum running families
stiff back aches
so that they were no longer able to sit
at the elbows of the president
with turkey muskets   or/ sit
on their behinds watching the boat races
off Massachusetts through field glasses but/
how they found their duck pants
   pulled off in the get-back-in-the-alleys
   of the world and/
how they were routed by the people
   spitting into their palms
   just waiting to use those lobster pinchers
   or smash that martini glass and/
how they warned him
               and gave him a chance
   with no behind the back dillinger
   killing by flat headed dicks but/
how they held megaphones
            in their fists
   saying   come out with your hands up and/

how refusing to believe the jig was up
   he accused them
                of apocalyptic barking
   saying out of the corner of his mouth
   come in and get me and/
how they snagged at his khaki legs
   until their mouths were full
   of ankles and calves and/
how they sank their teeth into his swanky jugular
   getting the sweet taste of max factor
   on their tongues and/
how his screams were so loud
   that the skins of eardrums blew off
   and blood trickled
             down the edges of mouths

and people got hip to his aliases/
                i mean/
democracy and freedom began bouncing
all over the world
      like bad checks
as people began scratching their heads
and stroking their chins
as his rhetoric stuck in his fat throat
    while he quoted
men with frills on their wrists

and fake moles on their cheeks
and swans on their snuff boxes
   who sit in Gilbert Stuart's portraits
   talking like baroque clocks/
   who sit talking turkey talk
    to people who say   we don't want
                   to hear it
as they lean over their plows reading Mao
wringing the necks of turkeys
   and making turkey talk gobble
   in upon itself
in Mekong and Danang and Santo Domingo
and

Che Guevara made personal appearances everywhere

Che Guevara in Macy's putting incendiary flowers
on marked down hats   and women
scratching out each other's eyes over ambulances
Che Guevara in Congress putting TNT shavings
in the ink wells   and politicians
tripped over their jowls trying to get away
Che Guevara in small towns and hamlets
where cans jump from the hands of stock clerks
   in flaming super markets/
where skyrocketing devil's food cakes
   contain the teeth of republican bankers/

where the steer of gentleman farmers
   shoot over the moon like beefy missiles
          while undeveloped people
stand in road shoulders saying
fly Che fly bop   a few for us
   put cement on his feet
   and take him for a ride

O Walt Whitman
visionary of leaking faucets
great grand daddy of drips
   you said I hear america singing
but/ how can you sing when your throat is slit
and O/ how can you see when your head bobs
   in a sewer
in Danang and Mekong and Santo Domingo

and look at them weep for a stiff/
                i mean
a limp dead hood
Bishops humping their backsides/
folding their hands in front of their noses
forming a human carpet for a zombie
men and women looking like sick dust mops/
   running their busted thumbs
   across whiskey headed guitars/

weeping into the evil smelling carnations
   of Baby Face McNamara
   and Killer Rusk
whose arms are loaded with hijacked rest
in peace wreaths and/
look at them hump this stiff in harlem/
sticking out their lower lips/
and because he two timed them/
   midget manicheans shaking their fists
   in bullet proof telephone booths/
   dialing legba on long distance
   receiving extra terrestrial sorry
                   wrong number
seeing big nosed black people land in space ships/
seeing swamp gas/
shoving inauthentic fireballs down their throats/
bursting their lungs on existentialist rope skipping/
   look at them mourn/
drop dead egalitarians and CIA polyglots
   crying into their bill folds
   we must love one another or die
while little boys wipe out whole regiments with bamboo
     sticks
while wrinkled face mandarins store 17 megatons in
     Haiku
for people have been holding his death birds

on their wrists and his death birds
make their arms sag with their filthy nests
and his death birds at their baby's testicles
and they got sick and fed up
with those goddamn birds
and they brought their wrists together and blew/

                                       i mean/

puffed their jaws and blew and shooed
   these death birds his way
and he is mourned by
drop dead egalitarians and CIA polyglots and
midget manicheans and Brooks Brothers Black People
   throwing valentines at crackers
     for a few spoons by Kirk's old Maryland engraved/
     for a look at Lassie's purple tongue/
     for a lock of roy rogers' hair/
     for a Lawrence Welk champagne bubble

as for me/ like the man said
i'm always glad when the chickens come home to roost

The Feral Pioneers
for Dancer

I rise at 2 a.m. these mornings, to
polish my horns; to see if the killing
has stopped. It is still snowing outside;
it comes down in screaming white
clots.

We sleep on the floor. I popped over
the dog last night & we ate it with
roots & berries.

The night before, lights of a
wounded coyote I found in
the pass.
(The horse froze weeks ago)

Our covered wagons be trapped
in strange caverns of the world.
Our journey, an entry in the thirty-
year old Missourian's '49 Diary.
    'All along the desert road from the
    very start, even the wayside was strewed
    with dead bodies of oxen, mules & horses
    & the stench was horrible.'

America, the mirage of a
naked prospector, with sand
in the throat, crawls thru
the stink.
Will never reach the Seven Cities.
Will lie in ruins of
once great steer.

I return to the cabin's
warmest room; Pope Joan is
still asleep. I lie down, my hands
supporting my head.

In the window, an apparition,
Charles Ives:
tears have pressed white hair
to face.

Instructions to a Princess
for Tim

it is like the plot of an ol
novel. yr mother comes down
from the attic at midnite & tries
on weird hats. i sit in my study
the secret inside me. i deal it
choice pieces of my heart, down
in the village they gossip abt
the new bride.
i have been saving all this
love for you my dear. if my
house burns down, open my face
& you will be amazed.

There's a Whale in my Thigh

There's a whale in my thigh. at
nite he swims the 7 seas. on
cold days i can feel him sleeping.
i went to the dr to see abt myself.
'do you feel this?' the dr asked,
a harpoon in my flesh. i nodded
yes in a clinic room of frozen
poetry.
'then there's no whale in yr thigh.'

there's a whale in my mind. i
feed him arrogant prophets.

I am a Cowboy in the Boat of Ra

'The devil must be forced to reveal any such physical evil
(potions, charms, fetishes, etc.) still outside the body
and these must be burned.' (Rituale Romanum, published
1947, endorsed by the coat-of-arms and introductory
letter from Francis cardinal Spellman)

I am a cowboy in the boat of Ra,
sidewinders in the saloons of fools
bit my forehead   like   O
the untrustworthiness of Egyptologists
who do not know their trips. Who was that
dog-faced man? they asked, the day I rode
from town.

School marms with halitosis cannot see
the Nefertiti fake chipped on the run by slick
germans, the hawk behind Sonny Rollins' head
or the ritual beard of his axe; a longhorn winding
its bells thru the Field of Reeds.

I am a cowboy in the boat of Ra. I bedded
down with Isis, Lady of the Boogaloo, dove
down deep in her horny, stuck up her Wells-Far-ago
in daring midday getaway. 'Start grabbing the
blue,' I said from top of my double crown.

I am a cowboy in the boat of Ra. Ezzard Charles
of the Chisholm Trail. Took up the bass but they
blew off my thumb. Alchemist in ringmanship but a
sucker for the right cross.

I am a cowboy in the boat of Ra. Vamoosed from
the temple i bide my time. The price on the wanted
poster was a-going down, outlaw alias copped my stance
and moody greenhorns were making me dance;
    while my mouth's
shooting iron got its chambers jammed.

I am a cowboy in the boat of Ra. Boning-up in
the ol West i bide my time. You should see
me pick off these tin cans whippersnappers. I
write the motown long plays for the comeback of
Osiris. Make them up when stars stare at sleeping
steer out here near the campfire. Women arrive
on the backs of goats and throw themselves on
my Bowie.

I am a cowboy in the boat of Ra. Lord of the lash,
the Loup Garou Kid. Half breed son of Pisces and
Aquarius. I hold the souls of men in my pot. I do
the dirty boogie with scorpions. I make the bulls
keep still and was the first swinger to grape the taste.

I am a cowboy in his boat. Pope Joan of the
Ptah Ra. C/mere a minute willya doll?
Be a good girl and
bring me my Buffalo horn of black powder
bring me my headdress of black feathers
bring me my bones of Ju-ju snake
go get my eyelids of red paint.
Hand me my shadow

I'm going into town after Set

I am a cowboy in the boat of Ra

look out Set   here i come Set
to get Set   to sunset Set
to unseat Set   to Set down Set

            usurper of the Royal couch
            —imposter RAdio of Moses' bush
            party pooper O hater of dance
            vampire outlaw of the milky way

Black Power Poem

A spectre is haunting america—
   the spectre of neo-hoodooism.
all the powers of old america have entered into a holy alli-
   ance to exorcise this spectre: allen ginsberg timothy
   leary
richard nixon edward teller billy graham time magazine the
new york review of books and the underground press.

may the best church win. shake hands now and come
out conjuring

Neo-HooDoo Manifesto

Neo-HooDoo is a "Lost American Church" updated. Neo-HooDoo is the music of James Brown without the lyrics and ads for Black Capitalism. Neo-HooDoo is the 8 basic dances of 19th-century New Orleans' *Place Congo*—the Calinda the Bamboula the Chacta the Babouille the Conjaille the Juba the Congo and the VooDoo—modernized into the Philly Dog, the Hully Gully, the Funky Chicken, the Popcorn, the Boogaloo and the dance of great American choreographer Buddy Bradley.

Neo-HooDoos would rather "shake that thing" than be stiff and erect. (There were more people performing a Neo-HooDoo sacred dance, the Boogaloo, at Woodstock than chanting Hare Krishna . . . Hare Hare!) All so-called "Store Front Churches" and "Rock Festivals" receive their matrix in the HooDoo rites of Marie Laveau conducted at New Orleans' Lake Pontchartrain, and Bayou St. John in the 1880s. The power of HooDoo challenged the stability of civil authority in New Orleans and was driven underground where to this day it flourishes in the Black ghettos throughout the country. Thats why in Ralph Ellison's modern novel *Invisible Man* New Orleans is described as "The Home of Mystery." "Everybody from New Orleans got that thing," Louis Armstrong said once.

HooDoo is the strange and beautiful "fits" the Black slave Tituba gave the children of Salem. (Notice the arm waving ecstatic females seemingly possessed at the "Pentecostal," "Baptist," and "Rock Festivals" [all fronts for Neo-HooDoo]). The reason that HooDoo isn't given the credit it deserves in influencing American Culture is because the students of that culture both "overground" and "underground" are uptight closet Jeho-vah revisionists. They would assert the American and East Indian and Chinese thing before they would the Black thing. Their spiritual leaders Ezra Pound and T. S. Eliot hated Africa and "Darkies." In Theodore Roszak's book—*The Making of a Counter Culture*—there is barely any mention of the Black influence on this culture even though its members dress like Blacks talk like Blacks walk like Blacks, gesture like Blacks wear Afros and indulge in Black music and dance (Neo-HooDoo).

Neo-HooDoo is sexual, sensual and digs the old "heathen" good good loving. An early American HooDoo song says:

> *Now lady I ain't no mill man*
> *Just the mill man's son*
> *But I can do your grinding till the mill man comes*

Which doesn't mean that women are treated as "sexual toys" in Neo-HooDoo or as one slick Jeho-vah Revisionist recently said, "victims of a raging hormone imbalance." Neo-HooDoo claims many women philosophers and theoreticians which is more than ugh religions Christianity and its offspring Islam can claim. When our theoretician Zora Neale Hurston asked a *Mambo* (a female priestess in the Haitian VooDoo) a definition of VooDoo the Mambo lifted her skirts and exhibited her Erzulie Seal, her Isis seal. Neo-HooDoo identifies with Julia Jackson who stripped HooDoo of its oppressive Catholic layer—Julia Jackson said when asked the origin of the amulets and talismans in her studio, "I make all my own stuff. It saves money and it's as good. People who has to buy their stuff ain't using their heads."

Neo-HooDoo is not a church for egotripping—it takes its "organization" from Haitian VooDoo of which Milo Rigaud wrote:

Unlike other established religions, there is no hierarchy of bishops, archbishops, cardinals, or a pope in VooDoo. Each oum'phor is a law unto itself, following the traditions of Voo-Doo but modifying and changing the ceremonies and rituals in various ways. Secrets of VooDoo.

Neo-HooDoo believes that every man is an artist and every artist a priest. You can bring your own creative ideas to Neo-HooDoo. Charlie "Yardbird (Thoth)" Parker is an example of the Neo-HooDoo artist as an innovator and improvisor.

Neo-HooDoo, Christ the landlord deity ("render unto Caesar") is on probation. This includes "The Black Christ" and "The Hippie Christ." Neo-HooDoo tells Christ to get lost. (Judas Iscariot holds an honorary degree from Neo-HooDoo.)

Whereas at the center of Christianity lies the graveyard the organ-drone and the cross, the center of Neo-HooDoo is the drum the ankh and the Dance. So Fine, Barefootin, Heard it Through The Grapevine, are all Neo-HooDoos.

Neo-HooDoo has "seen a lot of things in this old world."

Neo-HooDoo borrows from Ancient Egyptians (ritual accessories of Ancient Egypt are still sold in the House of Candles and Talismans on Stanton Street in New York, the Botanical Gardens in East Harlem, and Min and Mom on Haight Street in San Francisco, examples of underground centers found in ghettos throughout America).

Neo-HooDoo borrows from Haiti Africa and South America. Neo-HooDoo comes in all styles and moods.

Louis Jordon Nellie Lutcher John Lee Hooker Ma Rainey Dinah Washington the Temptations Ike and Tina Turner Aretha Franklin Muddy Waters Otis Redding Sly and the Family Stone B.B. King Junior Wells Bessie Smith Jelly Roll Morton Ray Charles Jimi Hendrix Buddy Miles the 5th Dimension the Chambers Brothers Etta James and acolytes Creedance Clearwater Revival the Flaming Embers Procol Harum are all Neo-HooDoos. Neo-HooDoo never turns down pork. In fact Neo-HooDoo is the Bar-B-Cue of

Amerika. The Neo-HooDoo cuisine is Geechee Gree Gree
Verta Mae's *Vibration Cooking*. (Ortiz Walton's Neo-HooDoo
Jass Band performs at the Native Son Restaurant in Berkeley,
California. Joe Overstreet's Neo-HooDoo exhibit will
happen at the Berkeley Gallery Sept. 1, 1970 in Berkeley.)

Neo-HooDoo ain't Negritude. Neo-HooDoo never been to
France. Neo-HooDoo is "your Mama" as Larry Neal said.
Neo-HooDoos Little Richard and Chuck Berry nearly suc-
ceeded in converting the Beatles. When the Beatles said
they were more popular than Christ they seemed aston-
ished at the resulting outcry. This is because although they
could feebly through amplification and technological sham
"mimic" (as if Little Richard and Chuck Berry were Loa
[Spirits] practicing ventriloquism on their "Horses") the
Beatles failed to realize that they were conjuring the music
and ritual (although imitation) of a Forgotten Faith, a tra-
ditional enemy of Christianity which Christianity the Cop
Religion has had to drive underground each time they
meet. Neo-HooDoo now demands a rematch, the referees
were bribed and the adversary had resin on his gloves.

The Vatican Forbids Jazz Masses in Italy
Rome, Aug. 6 (UPI)—The Vatican today barred jazz and pop-
ular music from masses in Italian churches and forbade young
Roman Catholics to change prayers or readings used on Sun-
days and holy days.
*   It said such changes in worship were "eccentric and*
arbitrary."

A Vatican document distributed to all Italian bishops did not refer to similar experimental masses elsewhere in the world, although Pope Paul VI and other high-ranking churchmen are known to dislike the growing tendency to deviate from the accepted form of the mass.

Some Italian churches have permitted jazz masses played by combos while youthful worshipers sang such songs as "We Shall Overcome."

Church leaders two years ago rebuked priests who permitted such experiments. The New York Times, *August 7, 1970.*

Africa is the home of the loa (Spirits) of Neo-HooDoo although we are building our own American "pantheon." Thousands of "Spirits" (Ka) who would laugh at Jeho-vah's fury concerning "false idols" (translated everybody else's religion) or "fetishes." Moses, Jeho-vah's messenger and zombie swiped the secrets of VooDoo from old Jethro but nevertheless ended up with a curse. (Warning, many White "Black delineators" who practiced HooDoo VooDoo for gain and did not "feed" the Black Spirits of HooDoo ended up tragically. Bix Beiderbecke and Irene Castle (who exploited Black Dance in the 1920s and relished in dressing up as a Nun) are examples of this tragic tendency.

Moses had a near heart attack when he saw his sons dancing nude before the Black Bull God Apis. They were dancing to a "heathen sound" that Moses had "heard before in Egypt" (probably a mixture of Sun Ra and Jimmy Reed played in the nightclub district of ancient Egypt's "The Domain of Osiris"—named after the god who enjoyed the fancy footwork of the pigmies).

The continuing war between Moses and his "Sons" was recently acted out in Chicago in the guise of an American "trial."

I have called Jeho-vah (most likely Set the Egyptian Sat-on [a pun on the fiend's penalty] Satan) somewhere "a party-pooper and hater of dance." Neo-HooDoos are detectives of the metaphysical about to make a pinch. We have issued warrants for a god arrest. If Jeho-vah reveals his real name he will be released on his own recognizance dehorned and put out to pasture.

A dangerous paranoid pain-in-the-neck a CopGod from the git-go, Jeho-vah was the successful law and order candidate in the mythological relay of the 4th century A.D. Jeho-vah is the God of punishment. The H-Bomb is a typical Jeho-vah "miracle." Jeho-vah is why we are in Vietnam. He told Moses to go out and "subdue" the world.

There has never been in history another such culture as the Western civilization—a culture which has practiced the belief that the physical and social environment of man is subject to rational manipulation and that history is subject to the will and action of man; whereas central to the traditional cultures of the rivals of Western civilization, those of Africa and Asia, is a belief that it is environment that dominates man. The Politics of Hysteria, *Edmund Stillman and William Pfaff.*

"Political leaders" are merely altar boys from Jeho-vah. While the targets of some "revolutionaries" are Laundromats and candy stores, Neo-HooDoo targets are TV the museums the symphony halls and churches art music and literature departments in Christianizing (education I think they call it!) universities which propagate the Art of Jeho-vah—much Byzantine Middle Ages Renaissance painting of Jeho-vah's "500 years of civilization" as Nixon put it are Jeho-vah propaganda. Many White revolutionaries can only get together with 3rd world people on the most mundane "political" level because they are of Jehovah's party and don't know it. How much Black music do so-called revolutionary underground radio stations play. On the other hand how much Bach?

Neo-HooDoos are Black Red (Black Hawk an American Indian was an early philosopher of the HooDoo Church) and occasionally White (Madamemoiselle Charlotte is a Haitian Loa [Spirit]).

Neo-HooDoo is a litany seeking its text
Neo-HooDoo is a Dance and Music closing in on its
    words
Neo-HooDoo is a Church finding its lyrics
Cecil Brown Al Young Calvin Hernton

David Henderson Steve Cannon Quincy Troupe
Ted Joans Victor Cruz N. H. Pritchard Ishmael Reed
Lennox Raphael Sarah Fabio Ron Welburn are Neo-
HooDoo's "Manhattan Project" of writing . . .

A Neo-HooDoo celebration will involve the dance music
and poetry of Neo-HooDoo and whatever ideas the
participating artists might add. A Neo-HooDoo seal
is the Face of an Old American Train.
Neo-HooDoo signs are everywhere!
Neo-HooDoo is the Now Locomotive swinging
up the Tracks of the American Soul.

Almost 100 years ago HooDoo was forced to say
Goodbye to America. Now HooDoo is
back as Neo-HooDoo
You can't keep a good church down!

The Neo-HooDoo Aesthetic

Gombo Févi

A whole chicken—if chicken cannot be had, veal will serve instead; a little ham; crabs, or shrimps, or both, according to the taste of the consumer; okra according to the quantity of soup needed; onions, garlic, parsley, red pepper, etc. Thicken with plenty of rice. (Don't forget to cut up the gombo or okra.)

Gombo Filé

Same as above except the okra is pulverised and oysters are used

Why do I call it "The Neo-HooDoo Aesthetic"?

The proportions of ingredients used depend upon the cook!

Sermonette

a poet was busted by a topless judge
his friends went to morristwn nj & put
black powder on his honah's doorstep
black powder into his honah's car
black powder on his honah's briefs
tiny dolls into his honah's mind

by nightfall his honah could a go go no mo
his dog went crazy & ran into a crocodile
his widow fell from a wall &
hanged herself
his daughter was run over by a black man
cming home for the wakes the two boys
skidded into mourning
all the next of kin's teeth fell out

gimmie dat ol time
                     religion
it's good enough
      for me!

Mojo Queen of the Feathery Plumes

Why do you want me to slap you
before I make love to you, then
wonder why I do you like I do?

Dark Lady at Koptos, strange lady
at Koptos, Mojo Queen of the
Feathery Plumes

Crawling, pleading and being
kittenish are no habits of the
world's rare cat; shut up in
the mind's dark cage; prowling
in a garden of persimmon, mangoes
and the long black python

Dark Lady at Koptos, strange lady
at Koptos, Mojo Queen of the
Feathery Plumes

When the hunter comes his gleaming
blue coat will galvanize him; his
pearls of sabre teeth will electrify
him; his avocado-green claws will
expose his guts

Dark Lady at Koptos, strange lady
at Koptos, Mojo Queen of the
Feathery Plumes

The scout will run back thru
the forest; 4 Thieves Vinegar
on his tail; the whole safari
not far behind his trail; the dolls
left behind will bare your face;
and the cloth on the bush will be
your lace; you are the jeweler's Ruby
that has fled its case

Dark Lady at Koptos, strange lady
at Koptos, Mojo Queen of the Feathery
Plumes

The cat was dying to meet you
in the flesh but you never came
he wanted you wild but you wanted
him tame, why is your highness afraid
of the night?

Dark Lady at Koptos, strange lady at Koptos
Mojo Queen of the Feathery Plumes

The Black Cock

for Jim Hendrix, HooDoo from his natural born

He frightens all the witches and the dragons in their lair
He cues the clear blue daylight and He gives the night its dare
He flaps His wings for warning and He struts atop a mare
for when He crows they quiver and when He comes they flee

In His coal black plumage and His bright red crown
and His golden beaked fury and His calculated frown
in His webbed footed glory He sends Jeho-vah down
for when He crows they quiver and when He comes they flee

O they dance around the fire and they boil the gall of wolves
and they sing their strange crude melodies and play their
weirder tunes and the villagers close their windows and
    the grave-
yard starts to heave and the cross won't help their victims and
the screaming fills the night and the young girls die with
open eyes and the skies are lavender light
but when He crows they quiver and when He comes they flee

Well the sheriff is getting desperate as they go their
    nature's way
killing cattle smothering infants slaughtering those who
    block their way

and the countryside swarms with numbness as their
    magic circle grows
but when He crows they tremble and when He comes
    they flee

Posting hex-signs on their wagons simple worried farmers pray
passing laws and faking justice only feed the witches brew
violet stones are rendered helpless drunken priests are
    helpless too
but when He crows they quiver and when He comes they flee

We have seen them in their ritual we have catalogued
    their crimes
we are weary of their torture but we cannot bring them down
their ancient hoodoo enemy who does the work, the trick,
strikes peril in their dead fiend's hearts and pecks their
    flesh to quick
love Him feed Him He will never let you down
for when He crows they quiver and when He comes they frown

Betty's Ball Blues

Betty took the ring
from her fabled Jellyroll
Betty took the ring
from her fabled Jellyroll
She gave it all to Dupree
and eased it on his soul

She climbed his ancient redwood
and sang out from his peak
She climbed his ancient redwood
and sang out from his peak
She thrilled his natural forest
and made his demon creep

She shook the constellations
and dazzled them cross his eyes
She shook the constellations
and dazzled them cross his eyes
She showered his head with quasars
and made his Taurus cry

China China China
Come blow my China horn
China China China

Come blow my China horn
Telegraph my indigo skyship
and make its voyage long

Betty touched his organ
made his cathedral rock
Betty touched his organ
made his cathedral rock
His worshippers moaned
and shouted, His
stained glass windows cracked

One night she dressed
in scarlet and threw
her man a Ball
One night she dressed
in scarlet and threw
her man a Ball
The Butlers came as
zombies, the
guests walked thru
the walls

Dupree he shot the
jeweler, She had him
under a spell,

Dupree he shot the
jeweler, She had him
under a spell

The calmest man in
Sing-Sing is happy
in his cell

The Wardrobe Master of Paradise

He pins the hems of Angels and
He dresses them to kill
He has no time for fashion
No money's in His till
You wont see Him in Paris
or in a New York store
He's the wardrobe master
of Paradise; He keeps right
on His toes

He works from ancient patterns
He doesn't mind they bore
His models have no measurements
His buyers never roar
He never cares to gossip
He works right on the floor
He's the wardrobe master
of Paradise; He keeps right
on His toes

The evil cities burn to
a crisp, from where His
clients go; their eyes
are blood red carnage, their

purpose never fluffed,
His customers total seven
they have no time to pose
He's the wardrobe master
of Paradise; He keeps right
on His toes

He does not sweat the phony
trends, or fashions dumb
decree; His style is always
chic and in, He never takes
a fee
In Vogue or Glamour or Harper's
Bazaar; He's never written up
He's the wardrobe master
of Paradise; He keeps right
on His toes

The ups and downs of Commerce
His shop will not effect:
the whims of a fickle market
the trifles of jet-sets
The society editor would
rather die than ask Him for
a tip; He sews uninterrupted
He isn't one for quips

His light burns in the pit-black night
I've never seen Him doze
He's the wardrobe master
of Paradise; He keeps right
on His toes

Catechism of d Neoamerican Hoodoo Church

a little red wagon for d black bureaucrat
who in d winter of 1967 when i refused to
deform d works of ellison & wright—his betters—
to accommodate a viewpoint this clerk thot irresistible,
did not hire me for d teaching job
which he invitd me to take
in d first place.

this is for u insect w/ no antennae, goofy
papers piling on yr desk—for u & others. where
do u fugitives frm d file cabinet of death get
off in yr attempt to control d artist?
keep yr programming to those computers u love so
much, for he who meddles w/ nigro-mancers
courts his demise!

i
our pens are free
do not move by decree, accept no memos
frm jackbootd demogs who wd exile our minds.
dare tell d artist his role, issue demands on
cultural revolution. 2 words frm china where an
ol woman sends bold painters to pick grasshoppers
at 3 in d a.m. w/ no tea, no cigarettes & no
beer, cause ol women like landscapes or portraits

of their husbands face. done 50 yrs ago. standing
on a hill. a god, a majesty, d first chairman.
o, we who hv no dreams permit us to say yr name
all day. we are junk beneath yr feet,
mosquito noises to yr ears, we crawl on our
bellies & roll over 3 times for u. u are
definitely sho nuff d 1 my man.

ii
is this how artists shd greet u?
isnt yr apartment by d river enough? d
trees in d park? palisades by moonlight is
choice i hear, arent u satisfid? do u
want to be a minister of culture? (minister, a
jive title frm a dead church!) dressd in a
business suit w/ medals on yr chest? hving
painters fetch yr short, writers doing yr taxes,
musicians entertaining yr mistresses, sculptors
polishing yr silverware, do u desire 4 names
instead of 2?

iii
   i do not write solictd
   manuscripts—oswald spengler said
   to joseph goebbels when askd to make a
   lie taste like sweet milk.

because they wrote d way they saw it, said
their prayers wrong, forgot to put on their number in d
a.m., got tore dwn in d streets & cut d fool:
men changd their names to islam & hung up d phone on them.
meatheaded philosophers left rank tongues of ugly mouth on
their tables. only new/ark kept us warm that summer. but
now they will pick up d tab. those dear dead beats who put
our souls to d wall. tried us in absentia before
some grand karate who hd no style. plumes on garveys hat
he was.

iv

word of my mysteries is getting around, do not cm
said d dean / invite cancelld to speak in our chapel
at delaware state. we hv checkd yr background. u make
d crucifixes melt. d governor cant replace them.
stop   stop   outlandish customer.

v

i am becoming spooky & afar you all. I
stir in my humfo, taking notes. a black cat
superstars on my shoulder. a johnny root dwells
in my purse, on d one wall: bobs picture
of marie laveaus tomb in st louis #2. it is
all washd out w/x . . . s, & dead flowers &
fuck Wallace signs. on d other wall:
d pastd scarab on grandpops chest, he was

a nigro-mancer frm chattanooga. so i got it
honest. i floor them w/ my gris gris. what
more do i want ask d flatfoots who patrol d beat
of my time. d whole pie? o no u small fry
spirits. d chefs hat, d kitchen, d right
to help make a menu that will end 2 thousand yrs
of bad news.

vi
muhammed? a rewrite man for d wrong daily
news. messenger for cons of d pharaohs court.
perry mason to moses d murderer & thief. pr man
for d prophets of SET. as for poets? chapt
26 my friends—check it out. it is all there in
icewater clear.

ghandi? middleclass lawyer stuck on himself.
freed d brahmins so they cd sip tea & hate cows.
lenins pants didnt fit too good,
people couldnt smoke in front of him, on d
train to petrograd he gv them passes to go
to d head.

d new houngans are to d left of buck rogers,
ok buck up w/yr hands. where did u stash
our galaxies?

vii
bulletin
    to d one who put our
art on a line. now odd shapes will nibble u.
its our turn to put u thru changes. to drop
dour walter winchells on u like, i predict
that tomorrow yr hands will be stiff. to d
one who gaggd a poet. hants will eat yr
cornflakes. golfballs will swell in yr jaws at noon.
horrid masks will gape thru yr window at dusk. it will
be an all day spectacular. look out now,
it is already beginning. to d one who strongarmd
a painter. hear d noise climbing yr steps? u will
be its horse. how does that grab u? how come u
pull d sheets over yr head? & last & least o cactus
for brains. u muggd a playwright, berkeley cal.
spring 68. We hv yr photos. lots of them. what
was that u just spat/up
a lizard or a spider?

viii
spelling out my business i hv gone
indoors, raking d coals over my liver,
listening to my stories w/ yng widow
brown, talking up a trash in bars (if
i feel up to it). doing all those things put down

in that odor of hog doodoo printd as
a poem in black fire. i caught d whiff of yr
stink thou sow w/ mud for thots. d next
round is on me. black halloween on d rocks.
straight no chaser.

down d hatch d spooks will fly/ some
will thrive & some will die/ by these
rattles in our hands/ mighty spirits
will shake d land.

so excuse me while i do d sooner toomer.
jean that is. im gone schooner to a meta
physical country. behind d eyes. im gone be.
a rootarmd ravenheaded longbeard im gone be.
a zigaboo jazzer teaching mountain
lions of passion how to truck.

ix
goodhomefolks gave me ishmael. how
did they know he was d'afflictd one'?
carrying a gag in his breast pocket, giving
a scene a scent of snowd under w/ bedevilment.
i am d mad mad scientist in love w/ d dark.
d villagers dont understand me. here they come
with their torches. there goes a rock

thru d window. i hv time for a few more hobbies:
making d cab drivers dream of wotan
cutting out pictures of paper murderers

like d ol woman w/ d yng face
or is it d yng woman w/ d ol face?
take yr pick. put it to my chest.
watch it bend. its all a big punchline
i share w/ u. to keep u in stitches.
& ull be so wise when their showstopper
comes:
 this is how yr ears shd feel
 this is what u shd eat
 this is who u shd sleep w/
 this is how u shd talk
 this is how u shd write
 this is how u shd paint
 these dances are d best
 these films are d best
 this is how u shd groom yrself
 these are d new gods we made for u
u are a bucket of feces before them.
we know what is best for u. bend down
& kiss some wood.
make love to leather, if u
dont u will be offd

x

& d cannd laughter will fade &
d dirty chickens will fly his coop
for he was just a geek u see.
o houngans of america—post this on yr
temples.

DO YR ART D WAY U WANT
ANYWAY U WANT
ANY WANGOL U WANT
ITS UP TO U/ WHAT WILL WORK
FOR U.

so sez d neoarmerican hoodoo
church of free spirits who
need no
monarch
no gunghoguru
no busybody ray frm d heddahopper planet
of wide black hats & stickpins. he was
just a 666* frm a late late show &
only d clucks threw pennies

*false prophet of the apocalypse

Why I Often Allude to Osiris

ikhnaton looked like
prophet jones, who brick
by brick broke up a
french chateau & set it
down in detroit. he was
'elongated' like prophet
jones & had a hairdresser's
taste.
ikhnaton moved cities for
his mother-in-law &
each finger of his hands
bore rings.

ikhnaton brought re
ligious fascism to egypt.

where once man animals
plants & stars freely
roamed thru each other's
rooms, ikhnaton came up
with the door.

(a lot of people in new york
go for him—museum curators

politicians & tragic mulattoes)
i'll take osiris any
time.
prefiguring JB he
funky chickened into
ethiopia & everybody had
a good time. osiris in
vented the popcorn, the
slow drag & the lindy hop.

he'd rather dance than rule.

My Thing Abt Cats

In berkeley whenever
black cats saw dancer &
me they crossed over to
the other side. alan &
carol's cat jumped over
my feet. someone else's
cat pressed its paw against
my leg, in Seattle it's
green eyes all the way.
"they cry all the time when
ever you go out, but when
you return they stop," dancer
said of the 3 cats in the back
yard on st mark's place, there
is a woman downstairs who makes
their sounds when she feeds them.
we don't get along.

Man or Butterfly

it is like lao tse's dream, my
strange affair with cities.
sometimes i can't tell whether
i am a writer writing abt cities
or a city with cities writing
abt me.
a city in peril, everything that
makes me tick is on the bum. all
of my goods and services are wearing
down. nothing resides in me anymore.
i am becoming a ghost town with not
even an occasional riot to perk me
up

       they are setting up a
       commission to find out what
       is wrong with me. i
       am the lead off witness

Hoodoo Poem in Transient

1nce a year marie laveau
    rises frm her workshop
    in st louis #2, boards
    a bus & rides dwn to
    the lake. she threw
    parties there 100 years
    ago.
    some
    lake

Monsters From The Ozarks

The Gollygog

The Bingbuffer

The Moogie

The Fillyloo

The Behemoth

The Snawfus

The Gowrow

The Spiro

The Agnew

Beware: Do Not Read This Poem

tonite, *thriller* was
abt an ol woman, so vain she
surrounded her self w/
    many mirrors

It got so bad that finally she
locked herself indoors & her
whole life became the
    mirrors

one day the villagers broke
into her house, but she was too
swift for them. she disappeared
    into a mirror
each tenant who bought the house
after that, lost a loved one to
    the ol woman in the mirror:
    first a little girl
    then a young woman
    then the young woman/s husband

the hunger of this poem is legendary
it has taken in many victims
back off from this poem

it has drawn in yr feet
back off from this poem
it has drawn in yr legs
back off from this poem
it is a greedy mirror
you are into this poem. from
   the waist down
nobody can hear you can they?
this poem has had you up to here
     belch
this poem aint got no manners
you cant call out frm this poem
relax now & go w/ this poem
move & roll on to this poem

     do not resist this poem
     this poem has yr eyes
     this poem has his head
     this poem has his arms
     this poem has his fingers
     this poem has his fingertips

this poem is the reader & the
     reader this poem

statistic: the us bureau of missing persons reports
   that in 1968 over 100,000 people disappeared
   leaving no solid clues
        nor trace   only
a space   in the lives of their friends

Dualism

In Ralph Ellison's Invisible Man

I am outside of
history. i wish
i had some peanuts, it
looks hungry there in
its cage

i am inside of
history. its
hungrier than i
thot

Guilty, the New York Philharmonic Signs Up a Whale

Today the New York
Philharmonic signed up
a whale.
Ortiz Walton is black
& better than Casals.
Well Ortiz, I guess you'll
have to swim the Atlantic

If my Enemy is a Clown,
a Natural Born Clown

i tore down my thoughts
roped in my nightmares
remembered a thousand curses
made blasphemous vows to demons
choked on the blood of hosts
   ate my hat
threw fits in the street
got up bitchy each day
told off the mailman
lost many friends
left parties in a huff
dry fucked a dozen juke boxes
made anarchist speeches in brad
the falcon's 55 (but was never
thrown out)
drank 10 martinis a minute
until 1 day the book was finished

my unspeakable terror between the
covers, on you i said to the
enemies of the souls

well lorca, pushkin i tried
but in this place they assassinate
you with pussy or pats on
the back, lemon chiffon between
the cheeks or 2 weeks on a mile
long beach.

i have been the only negro
on the plane 10 times this year
and its only the 2nd month
i am removing my blindfold and
leaving the dock. the judge
giggles constantly and the prosecutor
invited me to dinner

no forwarding address please

i called it pin the tail on the devil
they called it avant garde
they just can't be serious
these big turkeys

The Piping Down of God

god is above grammar
a monk once said. i
want to sit on the window
god told the ticket clerk. you
mean next to the window the
clerk corrected. no, on
the window god insisted. the
clouds have a right to
cheer their boss.

the clerk apologized
& god piped down.

Anon. Poster:

poor sam presents at

ESTHER'S ORBIT ROOM

1753–7th Street Oakland California
Reunion of Soul
with   the   Sensational   Team   of
Vernon & Jewel
(back together again)
music by
the   Young   Lyons

American Airlines Sutra

put yr cup on my tray
the stewardess said 40,000
feet up. (well i've
never done it that way. what
have i got to lose.)

i climb into a cab & the
woman driver is singing
along with Frank Sinatra
"how was your flight coming in?"

(another one. these americans,
only one thing on their
minds.)

The Inside Track

a longshot if he cracks up in
doors, but 2 to 1 he
flips out on tv. every
time nixon goes before the
cameras, 80,000 bookies
hold their breaths

For Cardinal Spellman Who Hated Voo Doo

sick
black grass will
grow on his plot and
the goats will eat
& choke on it

and the keeper of the children's
cries
will terrify his neighbors
& gravediggers
will ask for two weeks
off

when will the next one's
brain explode
or turn from meat to
rock

tomorrow
a week
a month from someday
or the next three turns
of the
moon

Dragon's Blood

just because you
cant see d stones dont
mean im not building.
you aint no mason. how
d fuck would you know.

Columbia

a dumb
figure
skater per
forming to
strauss'
*also spake
zarathustra.*

she stumbled
during the spin.

i saw this today
on wide wide
world of
sports.

no lie.

Treatment for Dance W/ Trick Ending

one cop enters a store
a 2nd cop pulls a cat frm a tree
a 3rd cop helps an ol woman across
   the street
a 4th cop slaps a prisoner

the cop who pulled the cat frm the
tree leaves the store with a package
& whistling walks dwn the street
the prisoner is put into a box away frm
his fellows
the ol woman files a complaint

one nite in 1965 at 3 in the AM i
stumble down second ave.
8 Cadillacs pull up in front
of ratner's. it is a shift of
the 9th precinct. coming on duty
the next morning the cobbler
awakes to find his shoes ruined

Back to Back: 3rd Eye
for D.H.

Who are you? Napoleon or something? Fresh from Elba, liberating the countryside? You wonder why cheering throngs don't turn out to greet you, in Oakland, in Richmond, in El Cerrito, behind the county courthouse on the telephone book. New York will follow you like a Westside meatpacking house that barters your heart for free ice. They keep to themselves out here.

Marlon Brando's silver hair sells
Up-America cakes on the weekends.

STOP!

Western Union for Zora Neale Hurston:
Moscow has fallen! Please wire Erzulie for triumphant march into the art!

Off d Pig

background:
   a reckoning has left
some minds hard hit. they blow,
crying for help, out to sea like
dead trees & receding housetops. i
can sympathize. i mean, all of us
have had our dreams broken over some
body's head. those scratched phono
graph records of d soul.
we
   all have been zombed along
d way of a thousand eyes glowing at midnite.
   our pupils have been vacant
   our hands have been icey &
   we have walked with d tell tale
   lurch
all of us have had this crisis of consciousness
which didnt do nobody no good
or a search for identity
which didnt make no never mind neither

at those times we got down on our knees & call
ed up the last resort. seldom do we bother him
for he is doing heavy duty for d universe. only

once has he been disturbed & this was to
   put some color into a woman's blues
he came like a black fire engine spun & sped
by khepera
he is very pressed for time &
do nots play

he apologises for being late
he rolls up his sleeves & rests his bird
he starts to say a few words to d crowd.
he sees d priests are out to lunch so he
just goes on head with what he got to do

out of d night blazing from ceciltaylorpianos
   Thoth sets down his fine black self
d first black scribe
d one who fixes up their art
d one who draws d circle with his pen
d man who beats around d bush
d smeller outer of d fiend

   jehovah-apep jumps up bad on d set
   but squeals as spears bring him down

a curfew is lifted on soul
friendly crowds greet one another in d streets

Osiris struts his stuff & dos d thang to words
    hidden beneath d desert

chorus—just like a legendary train that
    one has heard of but never seen
    broke all records in its prime
    takes you where you want to go right fast

    i hears you woo woo o neo american hoo doo church
    i hears you woo woo o neo american hoo doo church
    i hears you woo woo o neo american hoo doo church
    i hears you woo woo o neo american hoo doo church
    amen-ra   a-men ra   a-man ra

General Science

things in motion
hv a tendency to
stay in motion. the
most intelligent
ghosts are those
who do not know
they are dead:

something just
crossed my
hands

Report of the Reed Commission

I conclude that for
the first time in
history the practical
man is the loon and the
loon the practical man

a man on the radio just
said that air pollution
is caused by jelly fish.

What You Mean I Can't Irony?

A high-yellow lawyer woman
told me I ought to go to
Europe to "broaden your per
spective." This happened at
a black black cocktail party
an oil portrait, Andrew Carnegie,
smiling down

White Hope
for Shane Stevens

jack johnson licked
one pug so, d man
retired to a farm.
never again opened
his mouth save to
talk abt peachtrees
sow & last year's
almanac;

and whenever somebody
say jack johnson,

he'd get that far away
look.

Untitled 1

friday in berkeley. the crippled
ship has just returned frm
behind the moon. fools wave
flags on destroyers in the pacific
i am worried abt this dog
lying in the street. he wants
to get some sun. the old man
across the street trims his
rosebush while just 4 blocks
away there is a war. people
are being arraigned
fingerprinted
hauled away to st rita
made to lie on the floor
the newspapers will lie
abt all this. abt these
12 year olds throwing
stones at the cops, they
wanted to get at some sun
no matter what heavy
traffic was coming down
on them

Untitled II

that house has
a pall of bad
luck hovering over
head
i told you
not to go there
anymore. see
what you get?

Untitled III

everybody in columbia
heights speaks french
ever go to a party there?
bore you to tears.

Untitled IV

the difference between
my heart & your
intellect, my un
disciplined way of
doing
things (i failed
the written driver's
test for example)
& your science, is
the difference between
the earth &
the snow.

the earth wears its
colors well. builds them
loves them & sticks with
them

the snow needs no one.
it lies there all cold
like. it greases behind
wolftracks & wingless
dead birds.
it is a hardship on the poor

thinking is its downfall

Gangster Goes Legit

One day he became six eyes.
The tommy gun on the desk,
as many.
he went into the tommy gun
business

This Poetry Anthology I'm Reading

this poetry anthology
i'm reading reminds me
of washington d.c.
every page some marbled
trash. old adjectives stand
next to flagcovered coffins.
murderers mumbling in
their sleep.

in the rose garden the
madman strolls alone. the
grin on his face just
won't quit

Dress Rehearsal Paranoia #2

In san francisco they are
taking up a collection. if
the earthquake won't come
they'll send for it.

Paul Laurence Dunbar in The Tenderloin

Even at 26, the hush when
you unexpectedly walked
into a theatre. One year
after *The History of Cakewalk.*

Desiring not to cause
a fuss, you sit alone
in the rear, watching a re
hearsal.
The actors are impressed. Wel
don Johnson, so super at des
cription, jots it all down.

I dont blame you for
disliking Whitman, Paul.
He lacked your style, like
your highcollared mandalaed
portrait in hayden's
Kaleidoscope; unobserved,
Death, the uncouth critic
does a first draft on your
        breath.

Badman of the Guest Professor

for Joe Overstreet, David Henderson, Albert Ayler &
d Mysterious "H" who cut up d Rembrandts

i

u worry me whoever u are
i know u didnt want me to
come here but here i am just
d same; hi-jacking yr stagecoach,
hauling in yr pocket watches & mak
ing u hoof it all d way to
town. black bard, a robber w/ an
art: i left some curses in d cash
box so ull know its me

listen man, i cant help it if
yr thing is over, kaput,
   finis
no matter how u slice it dick
u are done. a dead duck all out
of quacks. d nagging hiccup dat
goes on & on w/out a simple glass
   of water for relief

ii

uve been teaching shakespeare for
20 years only to find d joke
    on u
d eavesdropping rascal who got it
in d shins because he didnt know
enough to keep his feet behind d cur
tains: a sad-sacked head served on a
platter in titus andronicus or falstaff
    too fat to make a go of it
    anymore

iii

its not my fault dat yr tradition
was knocked off wop style & left in
d alley w/ pricks in its mouth. i
read abt it in d papers but it was no
    skin off my nose
wasnt me who opened d gates & allowed
d rustlers to slip thru unnoticed. u
ought to do something abt yr security or
    mend yr fences partner
dont look at me if all dese niggers
are ripping it up like deadwood dick;
doing art d way its never been done. mak
ing wurlitzer sorry he made d piano dat

will drive mozart to d tennis
        courts
making smith-corona feel like d red
faced university dat has just delivered china
        some 50 e-leben h bomb experts

i didnt deliver d blow dat drove d
abstract expressionists to my ladies
linoleum where dey sleep beneath tons of
wax & dogshit & d muddy feet of children or
because some badassed blackpainter done sent
french impressionism to d walls of highrise
    lobbies where dey belong is not my fault
martha graham will never do d jerk
shes a sweet ol soul but her hips
cant roll; as stiff as d greek
statues she loves so much

iv
dese are d reasons u did me nasty
j alfred prufrock, d trick u pull
d in d bookstore today; stand in d
corner no peaches for a week, u lemon
u must blame me because yr wife is
ugly. 86-d by a thousand discriminating
saunas. dats why u did dat sneaky thing

i wont tell d townsfolk because u hv
to live here and im just passing thru

v

u got one thing right tho. i did say
dat everytime i read william faulkner i
go to sleep.

fitzgerald wdnt hv known a gangster if one
had snatched zelda & made her a moll tho
     she wd hv been grateful i bet

bonnie of clyde wrote d saga of suicide
sal just as d feds were closing in. it is
worth more than d collected works of ts
eliot a trembling anglican whose address
is now d hell dat thrilld him so
last word from down there he was open
ing a publishing co dat will bore d
devil back to paradise

vi

& by d way did u hear abt grammar?
cut to ribbons in a photo finish by
stevie wonder, a blindboy who dances
on a heel. he just came out of d slang
& broke it down before millions.
     it was bloody murder

vii

to make a long poem shorter—3 things

     moleheaded lame w/4 or 5 eyes

1) yr world is riding off into d sunset

2) d chips are down & nobody will chance yr i.o.u.s.

3) d last wish was a fluke so now u hv to re

turn to being a fish

p.s. d enchantment has worn off

dats why u didnt like my reading list—right?

it didnt include anyone on it dat u cd in

vite to a cocktail party & shoot a lot of

     bull—right?

so u want to take it out on my hide—right?

well i got news for u professor nothing—i

am my own brand while u must be d fantasy of

   a japanese cartoonist

a strangekind of dinosaurmouse

i can see it all now. d leaves

are running low. its d eve of

extinction & dere are no holes to

accept yr behind. u wander abt yr

long neck probing a tree. u think

its a tree but its really a trap. a

cry of victory goes up in d kitchen of

d world, a pest is dead. a prehis

toric pest at dat. a really funnytime
prehistoric pest whom we will lug into
a museum to show everyone how really funny
u are
   yr fate wd make a good
scenario but d plot is between u &
charles darwin.

as i said, im passing thru, just sing
ing my song. get along little doggie &
jazz like dat. word has it dat a big gold
shipment is coming to californy. i hv to
ride all night if im to meet my pardners
dey want me to help score d ambush

From the Files of Agent 22

a black banana
can make you high
bad apples can get
you wasted
the wrong kind of
grapes tore up
for days
and a rancid orange
plastered

know your spirits
before entering
strange orchards

Introducing a New Loa

as i conclude this Work, a great hydrogen cloud, twenty seven million miles long leisurely passes thru this solar system at 40,000 miles per hr. "The biggest thing yet seen in space." No one knows where it came from. Another galaxy? This solar system?

it took the small halo of another planet, out to make a rep for itself, to squeal on it. I claim it as my floating orphan. When i walked past the FM antenna just now, it called out my name. I respond to it. I call it the invisible train for which this Work has been but a modest schedule. A time-table subject to change. Greetings from the swinging HooDoo cloud; way up there, the softest touch in Everything; doing a dance they call

"The Our Turn"

CHATTANOOGA

Chattanooga

1

Some say that Chattanooga is the
Old name for Lookout Mountain
To others it is an uncouth name
Used only by the uncivilised
Our a-historical period sees it
As merely a town in Tennessee
To old timers of the Volunteer State
Chattanooga is "The Pittsburgh of
The South"
According to the Cherokee
Chattanooga is a rock that
Comes to a point

They're all right
Chattanooga is something you
Can have anyway you want it
The summit of what you are
I've paid my fare on that
Mountain Incline #2, Chattanooga
I want my ride up
I want Chattanooga

2

Like Nickajack a plucky Blood
I've escaped my battle near
Clover Bottom, braved the
Jolly Roger raising pirates
Had my near miss at Moccasin Bend
To reach your summit so
Give into me Chattanooga
I've dodged the Grey Confederate sharpshooters
Escaped my brother's tomahawks with only
Some minor burns
Traversed a Chickamauga of my own
Making, so
You belong to me Chattanooga

3

I take your East Ninth Street to my
Heart, pay court on your Market
Street of rubboard players and organ
Grinders of Haitian colors rioting
And old Zip Coon Dancers
I want to hear Bessie Smith belt out
I'm wild about that thing in
Your Ivory Theatre
Chattanooga
Coca-Cola's homebase
City on my mind

4

My 6th grade teacher asked me to
Name the highest mountain in the world
I didn't even hesitate, "Lookout Mountain"
I shouted. They laughed
Eastern nitpickers, putting on the
Ritz laughed at my Chattanooga ways
Which means you're always up to it

To get to Chattanooga you must
Have your Tennessee
"She has as many lives as a
cat. As to killing her, even
the floods have failed
you may knock the breath out of
her that's all. She will re-
fill her lungs and draw
a longer breath than ever"
From a Knoxville editorial—
1870s

5

Chattanooga is a woman to me too
I want to run my hands through her
Hair of New Jersey tea and redroot
Aint no harm in that
Be caressed and showered in

Her Ruby Falls
That's only natural
Heal myself in her
Minnehaha Springs
58 degrees F. all year
Around. Climb all over her
Ridges and hills
I wear a sign on my chest
"Chattanooga or bust"

6

"HOLD CHATTANOOGA AT ALL HAZARDS"——Grant to Thomas

When I tasted your big juicy
Black berries ignoring the rattle-
Snakes they said came to Cameron
Hill after the rain, I knew I
Had to have you Chattanooga
When I swam in Lincoln Park
Listening to Fats Domino sing
I found my thrill on Blueberry
Hill on the loudspeaker
I knew you were mine Chattanooga
Chattanooga whose Howard Negro
School taught my mother Latin
Tennyson and Dunbar
Whose Miller Bros. Department

Store cheated my Uncle out of
What was coming to him
A pension, he only had 6
Months to go
Chattanoooooooooooooooooooga
Chattanoooooooooooooooooooga
"WE WILL HOLD THE TOWN TILL WE STARVE"—Thomas to
  Grant

7

To get to Chattanooga you must
Go through your Tennessee
I've taken all the Scotsboros
One state can dish out
Made Dr. Shockley's "Monkey Trials"
The laughing stock of the Nation
Capt. Marvel Dr. Sylvanias shazam
Scientists running from light-
ning, so
Open your borders. Tennessee
Hide your TVA
DeSota determined, this
Serpent handler is coming
Through

Are you ready Lookout Mountain?

"Give all of my Generals what he's
drinking," Lincoln said, when the
Potomac crowd called Grant a lush

8
I'm going to strut all over your
Point like Old Sam Grant did
My belly full of good Tennessee
Whiskey, puffing on
A.05 cigar
The campaign for Chattanooga
Behind me

Railroad Bill, A Conjure Man

A HOODOO SUITE

Railroad Bill, a conjure man
Could change hisself to a tree
He could change hisself to a
Lake, a ram, he could be
What he wanted to be

When a man-hunt came he became
An old slave shouting boss
He went thataway. A toothless
Old slave standing next to a
Hog that laughed as they
Galloped away.
Would laugh as they galloped
Away

Railroad Bill was a conjure man
He could change hisself to a bird
He could change hisself to a brook
A hill he could be what he wanted
To be

One time old Bill changed hisself
To a dog and led a pack on his
Trail. He led the hounds around
And around.
And laughed a-wagging
His tail. And laughed
A-wagging his tail

Morris Slater was from Escambia
County, he went to town a-toting
A rifle. When he left that
Day he was bounty.
Morris Slater was Railroad Bill
Morris Slater was Railroad Bill

Railroad Bill was an electrical
Man he could change hisself into
Watts. He could up his voltage
Whenever he pleased
He could, you bet he could
He could, you bet he could

Now look here boy hand over that
Gun, hand over it now not later
I needs my gun said Morris Slater
The man who was Railroad Bill

I'll shoot you dead you SOB
let me be whatever I please
The policeman persisted he just
Wouldn't listen and was buried the
Following eve. Was buried the
Following eve. Many dignitaries
Lots of speech-making.

Railroad Bill was a hunting man
Never had no trouble fetching game
He hid in the forest for those
Few years and lived like a natural
King. Whenever old Bill would
Need a new coat he'd sound out his
Friend the Panther. When Bill got
Tired of living off plants the
Farmers would give him some hens.
In swine-killing time the leavings of
Slaughter. They'd give Bill the
Leavings of slaughter. When he
needed love their fine Corinas
They'd lend old Bill their daughters

Railroad Bill was a conjure man he
Could change hisself to a song. He
Could change hisself to some blues

Some reds he could be what he wanted
To be

E. S. McMillan said he'd get old
Bill or turn in his silver star
Bill told the Sheriff you best
Leave me be said the outlaw from
Tombigbee. Leave me be warned
Bill in 1893

Down in Yellowhammer land
By the humming Chattahoochee
Where the cajun banjo pickers
Strum. In Keego, Volina, and
Astoreth they sing the song of
How come

Bill killed McMillan but wasn't
Willin rather reason than shoot
A villain. Rather reason than
Shoot McMillan

"Railroad Bill was the worst old coon
Killed McMillan by the light of the
Moon

Was lookin for Railroad Bill
Was lookin for Railroad Bill"

Railroad Bill was a gris-gris man
He could change hisself to a mask
A Ziba, a Zulu
A Zambia mask. A Zaramo
Doll as well
One with a necklace on it
A Zaramo doll made of wood

I'm bad, I'm bad said Leonard
McGowin. He'll be in hell and dead he
    Said in 1896
Shot old Bill at Tidmore's store
This was near Atmore that Bill was
    Killed in 1896.
He was buying candy for some children
Procuring sweets for the farmers' kids

Leonard McGowin and R. C. John as
Cowardly as they come. Sneaked up
On Bill while he wasn't lookin.
Ambushed old Railroad Bill
Ambushed the conjure man. Shot him
In the back. Blew his head off.

Well, lawmen came from miles around
All smiles the lawmen came.
They'd finally got rid of
Railroad Bill who could be what
He wanted to be

Wasn't so the old folks claimed
From their shacks in the Wawbeek
Wood. That aint our Bill in that
old coffin, that aint our man
You killed. Our Bill is in the
Dogwood flower and in the grain
We eat
See that livestock grazing there
That Bull is Railroad Bill
The mean one over there near the
Fence, that one is Railroad Bill

Now Hollywood they's doing old
Bill they hired a teacher from
Yale. To treat and script and
Strip old Bill, this classics
Professor from Yale.
He'll take old Bill the conjure

Man and give him a-na-ly-sis. He'll
Put old Bill on a leather couch
And find out why he did it.
Why he stole the caboose and
Avoided nooses why Bill raised so
Much sand.

He'll say Bill had a complex
He'll say it was all due to Bill's
Mother. He'll be playing the
Dozens on Bill, this
Professor from Yale

They'll make old Bill a neurotic
Case these tycoons of the silver
Screen. They'll take their cue
From the teacher from Yale they
Gave the pile of green
A bicycle-riding dude from Yale
Who set Bill for the screen
Who set Bill for the screen

They'll shoot Bill zoom Bill and
Pan old Bill until he looks plain
Sick. Just like they did old Nat

The fox and tried to do Malik
Just like they did Jack Johnson
Just like they did Jack Johnson

But it wont work what these hacks
Will do, these manicured hacks from
Malibu cause the people will see
That aint our Bill but a haint of
The silver screen. A disembodied
Wish of a Yalie's dream

Our Bill is where the camellia
Grows and by the waterfalls. He's
Sleeping in a hundred trees and in
A hundred skies. That cumulus
That just went by that's Bill's
Old smiling face. He's having a joke
On Hollywood
He's on the varmint's case.

Railroad Bill was a conjure man
He could change hisself to the end.
He could outwit the chase and throw
Off the scent he didn't care what
They sent. He didn't give a damn what

They sent.

Railroad Bill was a conjure man

Railroad Bill was a star he could change

Hisself to the sun, the moon

Railroad Bill was free

Railroad Bill was free

The Kardek Method

No son, I dont wanta draw
I hung up my *Petro* in the Spring
of '68. Had got done with pick
ing notches; and what with the wing
ing and all, I ask you, was it
worth it?
So uncock your rod friend. Have
a sitdown.
While I stand back about 15 feet
think about some positive things. The
gals at the Road to Ruin Cabaret at the
end of the trail. The ranch in
Arizona you have your heart set
on.
Dont fret the blue rays emanating from
my fingers. They aint gonna cut you.
A-ha. Just as I thought. Your outside
aura looks a little grey. Your particles
cry the dull murmur of dying. I detect
a little green and red inside your
protecting sheet. You are here but
your ghost running cross a desert in a
greyhound. It bought a ticket to
No Place In Particular.

Swooooooooooooooooooosh!!

Yonder went the Combined Hand Pass

Feel Better?

Haitians

1

Fell the leader and
Confuse the pack
Nature's way, this
Shaggy, limping buffalo
Is downed by
Fanged schemers with plenty
Of time, a dry, crawling,
Beach fooled a Chief Whale into
Thinking it was a sea

2

We too are taken in like
Fishbelly, Mississippi in
Paris, no sooner had he
Arrived but here they come
The jackals
Camping about his favorite
Cafés
Mooching off of him, the Blackamoors
Bearing tales about him on
A greenback pillow to the
Crew-cutted sheik

Remember?
The Island of Hallucinations

3
The prospect of Bird going
Tenor made saxophones leap
Like it was a Wall Street crash
Many hornmen were wiped out

4
You know, I used to be a
Hyena, many grins ago
Before my cabin door, this
Morning, the naked rooster
In the Georgia Sea Islands our
Brothers and Sisters have a
Cure for this mess. They
Let the sun infuse the print
    Me too

Skirt Dance

i am to my honey what marijuana is
to tiajuana. the acapulco gold of her
secret harvest. up her lush coasts i
glide at midnite bringing a full boat.
(that's all the spanish i know.)

Kali's Galaxy

My 200 inch eyes are trained
on you, my love spectroscope
Breaking down your wavelengths
With my oscillating ear
I have painted your
Portrait: ermine curled about
Yonder's glistening neck

They say you are light-years
Away, but they understand so
Little

You are so near to me
We collide
Our stars erupt into supernovae
An ecstatic cataclysm that
Amazes astronomers

I enter your Milky Way
Seeking out your suns
Absorbing your heat
Circumventing your orbs
Radiating your nights

Once inside your heavens
I hop from world to world
Until I can go no longer
And Z out in your dust
Your new constellation
Known for my shining process
And fish-tailed chariot

Poison Light
for J. Overstreet

Last night
I played
Kirk Douglas to
Your Burt Lancaster. Reflecting
20 years of tough guys I
Saw at the Plaza Theatre in
Buffalo, New York. I can
Roll an L like Bogart
You swagger like Wayne

Ours was a bad performance
The audience, our friends
Panned it. The box office
Hocked the producers

We must stop behaving like
The poison light we grew on

Ancient loas are stranded
They want artfare home
Our friends watch us. They
Want to hear what we say

Let's face it

My eye has come a long way

So has your tongue

They belong on a pyramid wall

Not in a slum

("Dead End"; 1937)

The Decade that Screamed

    the sun came up
the people yawned and stretched
in rat traps whipping mildewed cats,
pomaded and braced in gold bathrooms of
baroque toilet boxes,
from chairs with paws,
from snuff cases,
from the puzzlement of round square rooms
they poured into the streets,
yelling down phantom taxi cabs,
jostling old men
blowing their noses with tired flags

some came in steel rickshaws
some in buicks
some on weird pack animals
talking extinct words
(linguists bought them kool aid)
some popped gum
some were carried
some grumbled
some fondled pistols
others in trench coats jotted down names
for the state   took photos

babies set up tents
and auctioned off errant mothers
jive oatmeal was flung at finger-wagging humanists
who drew up their hind legs and split for the cafés
covering their faces with *Les Temps Moderne*
with grapefruit and cherries

a famous editor was hanged on the spot for quoting
jefferson with almost no deliberation his credit cards
stamps line gauge correspondence and grey pages
slid towards the sewer

some sprinted
some bopped
some leaned on shaky lamp posts
others sat down
crossed their legs
and marveled
as the old men
talked of what was
talked of what is
talked of what is to come
talked crazy talk
toyed with their whiskers
threw difficult finger exercises at each other
(white lightning)

jumped like birds
jumped like lions
(yellow thunder)

a girl above   on a ledge toes over the edge
knees knocking teeth chattering

JUMP JUMP JUMP (millions of hands megaphoning
razored lips)

some danced
some sang
some vomited
stained themselves
pared fingernails

the moon came sick with old testament hang ups
people fought over exits
rain rain on the splintered girl
rain rain on deserted rickshaws, buicks
in certain rooms we ball our fists
"today in Cyprus, gunbattling"
in certain rooms we say   how awful
"today in Detroit, sniper fire"
rain rain on the splintered girl
rain rain on the baby auctioneers

The Katskills Kiss Romance Goodbye

1

After twenty years of nods
He enters the new regime
The machine guns have been
Removed from the block
The women don't wear anything
You can see everything

2

Hendrick Hudson's Tavern
Has slipped beneath the
Freeway where holiday drivers
Rush as if they've seen the
Hessian Trooper seeking his
Head

3

They get their goosebumps at
The drive-in nowadays, where
The Lady in White at Raven
Rock is Bette Davis and
Burton apes Major André
Hanging before the Haunted
Bridge

4

A New England historian has
Proof that King George wasn't
So bad.
Gave in to every demand
Donated tea to the American needy
Yankees are just naturally jumpy

5

Where once stood madmen
Buttonholing you
Gentlemen think of Martinis
On the train to Mount Vernon

6

R.I.P. old Rip
Cuddle up in your Romance
Your dog Wolf is dead
Your crazy galligaskins out
Of style
Your cabbages have been canned
Your firelock isn't registered
Your nagging wife became a
Scientist, you were keeping
Her down

7

Go back to the Boarded Up
Alley and catch some more winks
Dreaming is still on the house

Untitled

law isn't all
The drivers test
Says nothing about
dogs, but people
stop anyway

Antigone, This Is It
for Fred

Whatever your name, whatever
Your beef, I read you like I
Read a book
You would gut a nursery
To make the papers, like
Medea your Poster Queen
You murder children
With no father's consent

You map your treachery shrewdly,
A computer
Click clicking
As it tracks a ship
Headed for the Unknown
Making complex maneuvers
Before splashing down into
Mystery

Suppose everyone wanted it their
Way, traffic would be bottled up
The Horsemen couldn't come
There would be no beauty, no radio
No one could hear your monologues
Without drums or chorus

In which you are right
And others, shadows, snatching things

Fate, The Gods, A Jinx, The Ruling Class
Taboo, everything but you
All the while you so helpless
So charming, so innocent
Crossed your legs and the lawyer
Muttered, dropped your hankie
And the judges stuttered

You forgot one thing though, thief
Leaving a silver earring at the
Scene of a house you've pilfered
You will trip up somewhere
And the case will be closed

Standup Antigone,
The jury finds you guilty
Antigone, may the Eater
Of The Dead savor your heart
You wrong girl, you wrong
Antigone, you dead, wrong
Antigone, this is it

Your hair will turn white overnight

And the Devil Sent a Ford Pinto
Which She Also Routed

Sarah was banged &
Slammed & thrown &
Jostled, shook &
Shifted & ripped
& rumpled

D nex day she was on
D freeway

Tennesseeee women

   thoroughbreds

Cuckoo

A cuckoo is a funny bird
Ridiculously masked he will
Tickle your tummy with
His quill
He will look like you
And be your brother

He will cheep your old favorites
At the drop of your dime

A cuckoo is a silly thing
Until he eliminates your offspring
And splits your ears with
His origin

Rock Me, Baby

Turning Screw: In wave-guide
Technique an ad
Justing element in the form of
A rod whose depth of pene
Tration through the wall into
A wave-guide or cavity is ad-
Justable by rotating a screw

Mystery 1st Lady

franklin pierce's wife never
came downstairs.   she never
came upstairs either.

To a Daughter of Isaiah

I saw your drumming lover
On the tube last night
His wrists had been riveted
He made faces, like Jazz
Was a dentist
His gutbucket was
Straight from the Academy
That is, you couldn't
Grind to it
(Matthew Arnold, blowing
His nose)

He drummed, I summed
You up while helping white
Wine get better:
Your juicy Ethiopian art
Lips (my, my)
Your moans. What moans!
Even the ceiling over the bed
Got hard

This happened way back in a book
You were my daughter of Isaiah
I was your flail and crook

My Brothers

They come up here
Shit on my floor
Spill my liquor
Talk loud
Giggle about my books
Remove things from their
Natural places

They come up here
And crackle the snot-
Nosed sniggle about
My walk my ways my words

Signify about what is
Dear to me

My brothers
They come up here and
Hint at underhanded things
Look at me as if to
Invite me outside

My brothers
They come up here

And put me on the hot
Seat so I feel I am
Walking the last mile

My wrong, sorry, no
Manners brothers
I will invite them again
I must like it?

You tell me

Contest ends at midnight

The Vachel Lindsay Fault

All wines are
Not the same
Red, nor are
All Bloods

Nothing to
Brood about
But, nevertheless
A dud

Back to Africa

A Tartar Wolf
Spider
Spinning
From the ceiling

Instead of
Squashing
You look
It up

Swift, Tiny and Fine

He can climb vulgar
Like scooting up the
Side of a diamond
Discourse with a phoenix
Sail out to sea in a
Golden-brown doughnut
He can run a rodeo
With ants

  This man
Can make the M in Mc
Donald's a rainbow
Transpose a sonata from
Fiddle to trumpet
Run out to the back yard
Pick a plum, eat that
Plum, run back
Sit down, cross his
Legs, smile
Then hear that sonata
Before it's tooted

Good

What the heck
I'm sick of Roller Derby champeens

A hummingbird standing still in mid air,
Robert Haydn is The Great Aware

Crocodiles

A crocodile dont hunt
Him's victims
They hunts him
All he do is
Open he jaws

Al Capone in Alaska

or
hoodoo ecology vs the judeo-
christian tendency to *let em*
have it!

The Eskimo hunts
the whale & each year
the whale flowers for the
Eskimo.
This must be love baby!
One receiving with respect
from a Giver who has
plenty.
There is no hatred here.
There is One Big Happy
Family here.

American & Canadian Christians
submachine gun the whales.
They gallantly sail out &
shoot them as if the Pacific
were a Chicago garage on
St. Valentine's day

Visit to a Small College

you name your buildings after
John greenleaf whittier. you
left a great critic Nick Aaron
Ford waiting at the airport
for 3 hours. the room i
sleep in is scorching but
when i request an air
conditioner you think it
a joke.

"open the window," you chuckle.

you invited me here but
don't have my books on your
list, or in your
bookstore.

i landed in your town
at 12 midnite & sarah
pointed to the blood on the
moon.

that will teach me to
mark my omens. believing

in future ones and up
dating old ones.
let's see
the president dropped the first
baseball of the season last yr.
what does that portend?

The Atlantic Monthly, December 1970

*THE LAST STANZA OF WHICH IS A RUSSELLIAN
STANZA NAMED FOR ITS BEST CRAFTSMAN—
NIPSEY RUSSELL*

Many whiskey ads. More even than *The
New Yorker.* Not even the subtlety of
Coolidge, wearing Indian feathers but
Seagram's V.O. covers an entire page.
Does enamel prose drive its readers
to drink? Living in New York? Or
Commentary's exchange of letters be
tween Podhoretz and Kazin? Rapiers!
Stilettos! Letter knives used to open
linen envelopes, 19 stories above the
upper West Side.

Well what about us and our razors?
*The Rhythms, The Chicago Nation,
The Crescent Moons, The Pythons or
The Berkeley Boppers?* Man, we
Dukes and do we? Muhammad Ali rum
blers; Riders of the Purple Rage

Dear *Atlantic Monthly* Dec. 1970.

Is Augustus still the Emperor? Can
Rev. Billy Moyers dance on a dime?
Is that Ralph Ellison in Frank Sin-
atra's raincoat or Floyd Patterson
lifting several White Hopes from
the canvas? The album notes for
Strangers in the Night?
Well what did I expect? The multi
ple assassin theory of the *L.A.*
Free Press? E.V.O.'s hepatitis
yellow? The Dubious Achievements of
Esquire? The Schwarz is Beautiful
school teacher over at *Evergreen*
clinging to her English text?

You pays your dollar and you gets
Tabbed. Ah, that smooth velvet taste
We've come a long way from *Sneaky*
Pete, now hain't we? You know
we is

Confidentially though,
a young writer informed me that
this *Atlantic* issue made him
feel like Sugar Ray among the
Mormons. The black-as-Ham Utah

night when Sugar took off Gene
Fullmer's jaw. Never will for
get it. A left hook from out
of nowhere. And before his crafty
handlers could wise their boy to
the Sean O Casey shuffle and the
Mark Twain Possum, Fullmer had
done received his Baron Saturday
and was out cold on the floor.

"Why did they stop it? I'm not
hurt," the Kayoed Kid complain
ed. But it was too late, the sta
dium was empty, and Sugar was
on the train.

The Last Week in 30
for Victor Cruz on D Moon

5 before 2/22 i am
a magnified lizard in
a science fiction film. 1944
is when it was made; the
year ol men played volley
ball w/ children before add
ing them to the bones of
   europe

mother of dragons a swell
head said just as the ufo
carried him off. right
on time too; they signed his
happy papers d day befo. he
couldn/t keep his tongue
   still

i am spending my birthday in
a city built on junk left by
   a   glacier

a zoology professor/s wife jumped
off a bridge last week. that

fri he heard heavy breathing on
the other end of the line. the
news called it alienation

aint gon kill this cat. i
am moving into a new age. today
i broke the ice. my pulse begins to
move across a new world.

Loup Garou Means Change Into

If Loup Garou means change into
When will I banish mine?
I say, if Loup Garou means change
Into when will I shed mine?
This eager Beast inside of me
Seems never satisfied

I was driving on the Nimitz wasn't
Paying it no mind
I was driving on the Nimitz wasn't
Paying it no mind
Before you could say "Mr. 5 by 5"
I was doin 99

My Cherokee is crazy
Can't drink no more than 4
My Cherokee is crazy
Can't stand no more than 4
By the time I had my 15th one
I was whooping across the floor
I was talking whiskey talking
I was whooping across the floor

Well, I whistled at a Gypsy who was reading at my cards

She was looking at my glad hand when something came
Across the yard started wafting across the kitchen
Started drifting in the room, the black went out her
Eyeballs a cat sprung cross her tomb
I couldn't know what happened till I looked behind the
    door
Where I saw her cold pale husband
WHO'S BEEN DEAD SINCE 44

They say if you get your 30
You can get your 35
Folks say if you get to 30
You can make it to 35
The only stipulation is you
Leave your Beast outside

Loup Garou the violent one
When will you lay off me
Loup Garou the Evil one
Release my heart my seed
Your storm has come too many times
And yanked me to your sea

I said please Mr. Loup Garou
When will you drop my goat
I said mercy Mr. Loup Garou

Please give me victory
I put out the beans that evening
Next morning I was free

.05

If i had a nickel
For all the women who've
Rejected me in my life
I would be the head of the
World Bank with a flunkie
To hold my derby as i
Prepared to fly chartered
Jet to sign a check
Giving India a new lease
On life

If i had a nickel for
All the women who've loved
Me in my life i would be
The World Bank's assistant
Janitor and wouldn't need
To wear a derby
All i'd think about would
Be going home

The Author Reflects on His 35th Birthday

35? I have been looking forward
To you for many years now
So much so that
I feel you and I are old
Friends and so on this day, 35
I propose a toast to
Me and You
35? From this day on
I swear before the bountiful
Osiris that
If I ever
If I EVER
Try to bring out the
Best in folks again I
Want somebody to take me
Outside and kick me up and
Down the sidewalk or
Sit me in a corner with a
Funnel on my head

Make me as hard as a rock
35, like the fellow in
The story about the
Big one that got away

Let me laugh my head off
With Moby Dick as we reminisce
About them suckers who went
Down with the *Pequod*
35? I ain't been mean enough
Make me real real mean
Mean as old Marie rolling her eyes
Mean as the town Bessie sings about
"Where all the birds sing bass"

35? Make me Tennessee mean
Cobra mean
Cuckoo mean
Injun mean
Dracula mean
Beethovenian-brows mean
Miles Davis mean
Don't-offer-assistance-when
Quicksand-is-tugging-some-poor
Dope-under-mean
Pawnbroker mean
Pharaoh mean
That's it, 35
Make me Pharaoh mean
Mean as can be
Mean as the dickens
Meaner than mean

When I walk down the street
I want them to whisper
There goes Mr. Mean
"He's double mean
He even turned the skeletons
In his closet out into
The cold"

And 35?
Don't let me trust anybody
Over Reed but
Just in case
Put a tail on that
Negro too

Jacket Notes

Being a colored poet
Is like going over
Niagara Falls in a
Barrel

An 8 year old can do what
You do unaided

The barrel maker doesn't
Think you can cut it

The gawkers on the bridge
Hope you fall on your
Face

The tourist bus full of
Paying customers broke-down
Just out of Buffalo

Some would rather dig
The postcards than
Catch your act

A mile from the brink

It begins to storm

But what really hurts is
You're bigger than the
Barrel

A Secretary
to the Spirits

Pocadonia

You dragged me into your love pond
Pocadonia, your snapping turtle got the
best of me.
You dragged me into your love pond
Pocadonia, your snapping turtle got
the best of me
It was raining down on Hang-over morning
my head was in a sag
I looked over at your pillow
A crease was where you used to be

For one whole year after you left
I wouldn't hardly touch my food
For one skinny year after you left
I wouldn't hardly touch my food
lived on wheat chex and peanut butter
lived on crusty bread and rice

Slept on a cold cold floor for a mattress
Dressed in salt water crocodile skin
Slept on a cold cold floor for a mattress
Dressed in salt water crocodile skin
People would point at me and murmur
Whenever I'd leave my den

Caught catfish with my barehands
And breaded it Cedar Rapids style
Caught catfish with my barehands
and fried it Cedar Rapids style
My only form of diversion
Was the hoot owls who were hooting outside

Used to go up on Indian Mountain
Watch the Gold Coast ships come in
Used to go up on Indian Mountain
Watch the Gold Coast ships come in
Wondering where was my red-eyed Pocadonia
Wondering where was my baby's been

I see by the Magnavox
where they burn candles for you
on the beaches of Rio
Images of you on the finest pottery
All the school girls wear the shampoo
you wear
Your face on the national stamps like
the King's
The drunk plays your song on the
Seabird till three
Pocadonia, Pocadonia why have you
forgotten me?

You up there on television
doing your standard trance dance
the thirty-foot Indian Python
the one I gave you resting on
your shoulders like white wings
They done made you Ms. Spirit World

Pocadonia Pocadonia
Do you remember me?
As you ride next to your new Obeah
Three finger Jack of the Bugaboo trade
In his 1971 white Eldorado, eyes behind shades
Wearer of imitation leopard skin suits
He's made you his slave
He has a franchise on wing-tipped shoes
He's done turned your eye again

His rhythm section sounds like beer cans
Rattling from the rear of a wedding hearse
You always like them loud Pocadonia
Your bent for plaid men with their lucky Roots
Rabbit's foot $300.00 leather-pants skin tight
They love to show out at ringside
During the Ali-Frazier fight
Pocadonia, you have gone red on me again

Pocadonia, my love do you remember me
When they duppy you again please don't
Call on me
I'm like a full-up motel with a fabulous view
My dreams, they say, No Vacancy to you
I'm like a full-up motel with a fabulous view
My dreams, they say, No Vacancy to you

Poem Delivered Before Assembly of Colored People Held at Glide Memorial Church, Oct. 4, 1973, and Called to Protest Recent Events in the Sovereign Republic of Chile

In the winter of 1964 Pablo Neruda
Lifted 195 lbs of ragged scrawls
That wanted to be a poet and put
Me in the picture where we stood
Laughing like school chums

No little man ever lifted me like that

Pablo Neruda was a big man
It is impossible for me to believe that
Cancer could waste him
He was filled with barrel-chested poetry
From stocky head to feet and
Had no need for mortal organs
The cancer wasn't inside of Pablo Neruda
Cancer won't go near poetry
The cancer was inside ITT
The Cancer God with the
Nose of President Waterbugger
The tight-Baptist lips of John Foster Dulles

And the fleshy Q Ball head of
Melvin Laird
Dick Tracy's last victim

The Cancer God with the body
Of the rat-sucking Indian Plague Flea
All creepy transparent and hunched up
Stalks the South American copper
Country with its pet anaconda
It breathes and hollers like
All the Japanese sci fi monsters
Rolled into one: Hogzilla
Its excrescency supply the Portuguese
With napalm

The Cancer God is a bully who mooches up
Rational gentle and humanistic men
But when it picked a fight with the poet
It got all the cobalt-blue words it could use
And reels about holding in its insides

Do something about my wounded mother
Says President Waterbugger
Shambling across the San Clemente beach
Whose sand is skulls grinded
Do something about my wounded mother

Says the slobbering tacky thing
Pausing long enough from his hobby
Ripping-off the eggs of the world
Their albumen oozing down his American
Flag lapel, his bareassed elephant
Gyrating its dung-wings
Give her all of South America if she wants it
And if she makes a mess
Get somebody to clean it up
Somebody dumb
A colonel who holds his inaugural address
Upside down and sports
Miss-matched socks

And if they can't stomach their
New leaders' uglysucker French
Angel faces then cover them up with
A uniform or hide its Most Disgusting
In a tank
Cover it up like they want to cover
Me up those pitiful eyes gazing from
The palm tree freeway of the Dead War
President Waterbugger your crimes
Will not leave office
No imperial plastic surgeon can
Remove them from your face

They enter the bedroom of your
Hacienda at night and rob you
Of your sleep
They call out your name

President Waterbugger
Next to you Hitler resembles
A kindergarten aide
Who only wanted to raise some geese
And cried when listening to
Dietrich Fischer-Dieskau
Everything you put your paws on
Becomes all crummy and yukky
In New Jersey the mob cries for Jumboburgers
In Florida the old people are stealing Vitamin E

President Waterbugger only your crimes
Want to be near you now
Your daughters have moved out of town
Your wife refuses to hold your hand
On the elevator
Inexplicably, Lincoln's picture
Just fell from the wall
Next time you kill a poet
You'd better read his poems first
Or they will rise up and surround you

Like 1945 fire cannons a few miles from
Berlin
And History will find no trace of
Your ashes in the bunker of your hell

A Secretary to the Spirits

The following minutes were
logged by this Secretary to
the Spirits during the last five
years which have occasionally been
like a devil woman on a heart

Sometimes I felt
only a beetle could inch up
from this situation
Y'awl know what I mean

I am no beetle
not even a bishop
got 90% wrong on the priest's
exam
Scared of snakes

Just a red baboon with the
hurricane's eye
got up sometimes in a Businessman's
three-piece
Mostly an errand boy for the spirits
It's honest Work
You can even come by promotions

I'll rise or
maybe grow up even

I hail from a long line of
risers
like Grand ma ma, old oak
off on a new path
she sculpts from the clay

Sather Tower Mystery

Seems there was this Professor
a member of what should be called
The Good German Department

Must have signed his name to
5,000 petitions in front of
the Co-op on Cedar
and bought two tons of benefit
cookies
Blames Texas for the sorry
state of the oceans
Rode a Greyhound bus "Civil
Rights," Alabama, 1960
Found the long yellow war
"deplorable"
Believes John "Duke" Wayne's
values to be inferior to his

He said, "Ishmael, I'd
love to do the right thing
for as you know I'm all for
the right thing and against
the wrong thing, but
these plaster of paris busts
of deceased Europeans

Our secret ways
Our sacred fears

"These books, leather-bound
'copyright 1789'
All of these things, precious
to me, gleaming like the
stainless steel coffee urn in
the faculty club, an original
Maybeck, 1902

"I'd stand up for Camelot
by golly, even if it meant
shooting all the infidels in
the world," he said
reaching into his desk drawer

"Why, I might even have to
shoot you, Ishmael"

Staring down the cold
tunnel of a hard .38
I thought

Most people are to the right
when it comes to where they must
eat and lay their heads!

Foolology

Shaken by his bad press, the wolf
presses north, leaving caribou to
the fox,
Raven, the snow player gets his
before buzzards with bright red
collars move in to dine near the
bottom of a long scavenger line

This poem is about a skunk, no
rather about a man, who though
not of the skunk family uses
his round-eye the way skunks do

After he eats, his friends eat
He is a fool and his friends are
fools but sometimes it's hard to
tell who is the biggest fool this
fool or his fool friends

By the time they catch us
we're not there
We crows
Nobody's ever seen a dead crow
on the highway

First moral: Don't do business
with people for whom April first
is an important date
they will use your bank balance to
buy eight thousand pies, tunics,
ballet slippers with bells and
a mail order lake in the middle of
a desert for splash parties

Second moral: Before you can spot the
fools in others you must rid yourself
of the fool in you
You can tell a fool by his big mouth

The Return of Julian the Apostate to Rome

Julian
Come back
It can't be long
For the emperor

He sees plots everywhere
Has executed three postmen
Rants in print against his
Former allies
Imagines himself a
Yoruba god
Has asked the Bishops to
Deify him

Not only is he short
He's nuts

Julian come back
The people are crapping
In the temples
Barbarian professors
Are teaching one god
They are ripping the limbs
Off our fetishes

They are carving the sea
Monsters from our totems
They made a pile of our
Wood sculpture and set fire
To it

Julian
Come back
Rude hags
Have crashed the senate
And are spitting on the
Elders

Meanwhile, Julian
The perennial art major
Ponders in the right wing
Of the monastery museum

The Egyptian collection

Sputin

Like Venus
My spin is retrograde
A rebel in more ways than one

I click my heels
In seedy taverns
& pinch the barmaids
On the cheeks

Madeira drips from
My devilish beard
My eyes sparkle dart
Flicker & sear
Man, do I love to dance

Something tells me the
Tzar will summon me to
Save his imperial hide

I peeped his messenger
Speeding through the gates of
The Winter Palace

He's heading this way

Soon, my fellow peasants will
See me in the Gazette
Taking tea with the royal family

They'll say
That crazy bum?

Sky Diving

"It's a good way to live and
A good way to die"
From a Frankenheimer video about
Sky diving
The hero telling why he liked to

    The following noon he leaped
    But his parachute wasn't with him
    He spread out on the field like
    Scrambled eggs

Life is not always
Hi-lifing inside
Archibald Motley's
"Chicken Shack"
You in your derby
Your honey in her beret
Styling before a small vintage
Car

Like too many of us
I am a man who never had much
Use for a real father
And so when I'm heading

For a crash
No one will catch me but
Me

The year is only five days old
Already a comet has glittered out
Its glow sandbagged by
The jealous sun

    Happens to the best of us
    Our brilliance falling off
    Like hair from Berkeley's roving
    Dogs

Even on Rose Bowl day
An otherwise joyous occasion
A float veered into the crowd
Somebody got bruised over the incident
Like a love affair on second ave.

It's a good lesson to us all
In these downhill days of a
Hard-hearted decade
Jetting through the world
Our tails on fire

You can't always count
On things opening up for you
Know when to let go
Learn how to fall

Soul Proprietorship

I

Billy Eckstine, now I
understand why you
went solo, even if it meant crooning
the Pastrami and Rye circuit from
Miami to Grossinger's
Maybe you got tired of babysitting
for other people's tubas, or
running out for reeds
Maybe you got tired of the
spitballs breaking the skin
of your neck while in the midst
of one of those ostentatious supper-
club bows
The bounced checks and half-empty
seats were hard on your dignity
and the bad publicity you received
from the black eye you gave your
agent, co-hort in a secret
deal with management
didn't help

II

You always had to put ice packs

on the lead tenor's head in Chicago
when by late afternoon a concert
was scheduled for Detroit
And there was always the genius
He was avant garde
which meant he had trouble playing
in scales of five flats
he spurned your attempts to
teach him things and went out
to organize his own band
They called their bloopers "new
music" and drew "experimental"
customers

customers who never smiled
and owned high blood pressure
When you travel single you
can take time out to catch up
with the funnies
You no longer have to order
40 cups of coffee
10 black
5 with cream, and
12 regular
You no longer have to keep

tabs on the two guys who wanted

tea

III

And when your only companion became

your thought

You came up with the Billy Eckstine

Shirt

With prints as beautiful as

the handle of an Islamic sword

and you made a million silver dollars

And you bought an old Spanish mansion

in California whose

wings could be seen from the sea

They look like two shining silver

collars, billowing, for lift off

Vamp

No wonder the vampire
Is dead
From the hem of his
Cloak to the roots of
His fangs he is one big
Dummy

  Doesn't he
Know that creeping
Through the open windows
Of people's lives can
Lead to his extinction?
Carrying off peoples'
Dear ones can get him stuck

  You can't even
Stake the stud without
Becoming caked in his
Blood

  There is a vampire
Who is cutting into
My orderly progression
In my profession

He shadows me about the
Country like an itinerant
Snake
Everything I do, It do

   He converts my
Friends into his concoctions
And convinces peasants that
I am their devil
He is putting ignorant
Heat on me

A wicked trick is dying
For me to use it
I can't hold out much longer
Vampire
In my sleep I hear you screaming
Vamp

Wise up Blood Sucker
Or you will have the
Dawn you hate

Sixth Street Corporate War

Not all rats live in sewers
Some of them dwell in 100,000 dollar
rat's nests on the Alameda
and drive to work in a Mercedes
laboratory rat white
You wouldn't even know they were
rats
on the mailbox it says Mr. Rodent

As big as a coffee table book
(The only book in the house)
he spends his time nibbling ratboy
in a rathouse with its
cheesy rat kitchen or scampering
on a rat sofa or in a bed of
rats
Or you might find him at the Ratskeller
wetting his rat whiskers on
rat soup
"my favorite drink" said
This shareholder rat there he
go old bureaucratic rat investor
in rattraps where people live
like rats

As years went by he gained more
status until he became the esteemed
Doctor Rattus
Crashed a tomcat convention and
demanded to be put on the
banquet
This even woke up Scrounger
or Mr. All Claws,
the toastmaster tomcat
catnapping on the dais
after a night of pre-
convention howling
"whaddya say, boys"
said the thrice decorated
rat scrapper
"rat cocktail
rat of the day
rat a la carte
or rat mousse?"

The other cats being
democrats cast their
votes by secret ballot
gulp!

Poetry Makes Rhythm in Philosophy

Maybe it was the Bichot
Beaujolais, 1970
But in an a.m. upstairs on
Crescent Ave. I had a conversation
with K.C. Bird

   We were discussing
rhythm and I said
"Rhythm makes everything move
the seasons swing
it backs up the elements
Like walking Paul-Chamber's fingers"

   "My worthy constituent"
Bird said, "The Universe is a
spiralling Big Band in a
polka-dotted speakeasy,
effusively generating new light
every one-night stand"

We agreed that nature can't
do without rhythm but rhythm can
get along without nature

This rhythm, a stylized Spring
conducted by a blue-collared man
in Keds and denims
(His Williamsville swimming pool
shaped like a bass clef)
in Baird Hall
on Sunday afternoons
Admission Free!

All *harrumphs!* must be
checked in at
the door

I wanted to spin
Bennie Moten's
"It's Hard to Laugh or Smile"
but the reject wouldn't automate
and the changer refused to drop
"Progress," you know

Just as well
because Bird vanished

A steel band had
entered the room

Untitled

Today I feel bearish
I've just climbed out of
A stream with a jerking
Trout in my paw

Anyone who messes with
Me today will be hugged
And dispatched

The Reactionary Poet

If you are a revolutionary
Then I must be a reactionary
For if you stand for the future
I have no choice but to
Be with the past

Bring back suspenders!
Bring back Mom!
Homemade ice cream
Picnics in the park
Flagpole sitting
Straw hats
Rent parties
Corn liquor
The banjo
Georgia quilts
Krazy Kat
Restock

The syncopation of
Fletcher Henderson
The Kiplingesque lines
of James Weldon Johnson
Black Eagle

Mickey Mouse
The Bach Family
Sunday School
Even Mayor La Guardia
Who read the comics
Is more appealing than
Your version of
What Lies Ahead

In your world of
Tomorrow Humor
Will be locked up and
The key thrown away
The public address system
Will pound out headaches
All day
Everybody will wear the same
Funny caps
And the same funny jackets
Enchantment will be found
Expendable, charm, a
Luxury
Love and kisses
A crime against the state
Duke Ellington will be

Ordered to write more marches
"For the people," naturally

If you are what's coming
I must be what's going

Make it by steamboat
I likes to take it real slow

Rough Trade Slumlord Totem

Here's how you put your enemy
atop a totem where the scavengers
get at him

This is for you, dummy
who hoarded our writings in
your basement, four solid months
like your brother landlord of
Sitka, Alaska, who chopped-up
the Tlingit totems for bar-b-cue chairs

The Raven will get you sucker
The Raven will hunt you down
Gaaaaaa! Gaaaaaaa! sucker

The thunder will empty its
bladder on your face you
seal-cow man who wobbles on
his belly with common
law fish in his mouth

May seagulls litter your
Punch-and-Judy corked eyes
May the eagle mistake your

snout for a mouse and sink
its claws into it
May the paint used on your
head be slum lord paint bound
to peel in a short time

And when you crash I hope
your landing place be
a maggot's hunting party
And while the rest of the
totem journey's into mother
soil
your segment remains
your sideshow providing
Laughing Forest
with a belly full

Tea Dancer Turns Thirty-nine

They will swoon no more his
four o'clock afternoons,
He bids farewell to his taxi
dancing heart throbs
He donates his clicks to the
Boogie Hall of Fame
Roll on Mississippi Roll on

From Beyond, cognac-voiced
Bojangles sent him El Rito
strawberries covered with Jack
Frost sugar, big as peaches!

A gesture from a man who could
Essence so, God ringed Satan to
wish him Happy Birthday

    Not too far back
his silver medals danced in
the brightest hock windows of
Bret Harte Boardwalk.
Now, it's caviar omelettes at
number one Fifth Ave

What changed his luck?

The little lady he calls his
Tiger Balm, the one beneath a Coit
Tower, half way up from Half Moon
Bay?

He hurries to her
Her red dragon in his eyes
red as the red trees of Modesto
red as the red in the red bridge of
death
Moon Ocean red

Colorwheels light upon Filipino gazers
in the Palace of Old Tokyo town their
wriggling rumps rooting for Donald Byrd
and the Black Byrds while just across town
romance has been replaced by shrunken jeans
You look like a sack, he said, before she
hurled chocolate milk at his white
European double-breasted suit

An embarrassing situation for the Order
of the Golden Bear, on the other side
of the Bay Bridge, having to negotiate

with lucky Feet who tripped them up
like the accidental hero in the Bank Dick
He spilled ashes all over the Queen's
Thug rug
She could do nothing but smile her
Silver-Jubilee smile, an outrage
to the civilized world
Would your majesty jern me in a game
of chanct? he said, sweeping his big
hairy floor-length arms and flipping
drumsticks to the ceiling
Will crocodiles reach Kampala this
year, or the Taj Mahal yellow?

They laughed at his blue serge suit
Dobbs crumpled from being sat on
but when he fired a revolver into
the cushion, they knew he wasn't
kidding

    And then there was the
Tea Dancer's march when the old ones
put the young set to shame with their
glides, kneebends, squats and
twirls

These days you have to have a Ph.D.
In the old days all you had to do was
dance

We mount our old days next to our stuffed
shoes and feed them wines only popes used
to drink

He's a spin around fool and his eyes are
kind of hazy but that don't mean he's lazy
if anything it means he's crazy
Give him a thousand dollars and he'll
sign off his professional frog's legs
(a minute of silence for Legs Diamond,
tea dancer, slain in Niagara Falls phone
booth—most people run out of steam—
tea dancers run out of dimes)

He doesn't know the difference between
his golden slippers and Stacey Adams
continued Fast Foods, the Boss
I ought to know, I run a factory full
of dead horses
when I'm not killing television

He thought of what Leslie Laguna said

in the Hotel Loretto up near Santa
Fe way, about why hares are heroines
in trickster tales
Because they're quick! she said
The Quick and the Dead

And so from the Papyrus Room
of the Pyramid Hotel
high above the River Nile of
his dream
Let's spin out some to
a crackling bundle
of Tennessee two-fisted
aqua-eyed fire
Born in grand old Oakland
on the day of six twos
Her smile spanned the delivery room

Finally, this item
today is the seventh
day of the seventh month
of the seventy-seventh year
of this century

Apples grow on trees!

POINTS OF VIEW

For Dancer

When lovers die they blossom
grapes
That's why there's so much
wine in love
That's why I'm still drunk
on you

Earthquake Blues

Well the cat started actin funny
and the dog howled all night long
I say the cat started actin very frightful
and the birds chirped all night long
The ground began to rumble
As the panic hit the town.

Mr. Earthquake Mr. Earthquake
you don't know good from bad
Mr. Earthquake Mr. Earthquake
you don't know good from bad
You kill the little child in its nursery
You burn up the widow's pad

The buildings started swaying
like a drunk man walking home
The buildings started swaying
like a drunk man walking home
The people they were running
and the hurt folks began to moan

Mr. Earthquake Mr. Earthquake
you don't know good from bad
Mr. Earthquake Mr. Earthquake

you don't know good from bad
You kill the little child in its nursery
You burn up the widow's pad

I got underneath my table
Had my head between my knees
I got underneath the table
Had my head between my knees
The dishes they were rattlin
and the house was rockin me

Mr. Earthquake Mr. Earthquake
you don't know good from bad
Mr. Earthquake Mr. Earthquake
you don't know good from bad
You kill the little child in its nursery
You burn up the widow's pad

I was worried about my baby
Was she safe or was she dead
I was worried about my baby
Was she safe or was she dead
When she phoned and said I'm
ok, Daddy. Then I went on back
to bed.

Mr. Earthquake Mr. Earthquake
you don't know good from bad
Mr. Earthquake Mr. Earthquake
you don't know good from bad
You kill the little child in its nursery
You burn up the widow's pad

Points of View

I
The pioneer stands in front of the
Old pioneer's home with his back-pack
walking stick and rifle
Wasn't me that Kisadi Frog-Klan
Indian was talking about when he
mentioned the horrors of Alaska
What horrors of Alaska?
Why Baranof was a swell fellow
Generous to the Indians, he was
known as far south as California
for his good deeds
Before we came the Indians were
making love to their children and
sacrificing their slaves, because
the Raven told them so, according
to them
"They couldn't even speak good
English and called the streams and
the mountains funny names
They were giving each other refrigerators
the potlatches had become so bad

We made them stop
They'd build a canoe abandon
it, then build another
We made them stop that, too
Now they have lawyers
They can have anything they want
If they want to go whaling
when we know they don't need to
go whaling
The lawyers see to it that they
go whaling
They're just like us
They buy frozen snow peas
just like we do
They're crazy about motorcycles
Just like we are

We brought them civilization
We brought them penicillin
We brought them Johnny Carson
Softball
We brought them trailer camps
They'd get married at fourteen
and die at 24
We brought them longevity

II

They brought us carbon dioxide
They brought us contractors
We told them not to dig there
They were clawed by two eagles
While uncovering the graves of
two medicine men

The white man has the mind of a
walrus's malignant left ball
We don't think the way they do
They arrive at the rate of one
thousand per month in cars
whose license plates read
texas oklahoma and mississippi
They built the Sheffield Hotel on
a herring bed
Everywhere are their dogs
Everywhere are their guns
Everywhere are their salmon-faced
women who get knocked up a lot
and sometimes enter the Chanel
restaurant wearing mysterious black
eyes, socked into their Viking-eyes
by men whose hair is plastered with
seal dung

It all began when
Chief Kowee of the Raven Klan showed
Joe Juneau the location of the gold
Now Mount Juneau is as empty as
a box of popcorn on the floor of
a picture show
When our people saw the first
Russian ship, we thought it was
the White Raven's return
Instead it was the Czarina's pirate
Dressed in Russian merchant's clothes
and a peacock's hat.
He shot Katlian in the back

The Ballad of Charlie James

I
Hunter's Point: Night
Papa Charlie James awakes
to see the 'Frisco police
at the foot of his bed
"Bring them hands from
underneath them sheets so's
we can see them. Let us see
what you got beneath those
sheets," they said, shooting
seventeen rounds of ammunition
into Charlie's bed

II
He survived the crazy rhythms
in his chest
his lungs whistling like
ghost winds, but he couldn't
survive the police
Hazardous to your health
if you are poor, Indian, or
Chicano, or if you're a sixty
year old black man asleep in
bed "Bring them hands from

underneath those sheets so's we can
see them, let us see what you got
beneath those sheets"

Like in Count Albuquerque's
town, where underneath the freeway
a lone woman wears "I Want Your Body"
on her t-shirt, a black man can get
shot for just horsing around
They use the redman for target
practice, they hang the Mexican
in jail.
O ain't it a shame what they did
to poor Charlie James. Have mercy
and ain't it a shame
"He just played dominoes
drank soda water, and looked
out the window" his neighbors said
Thinking of his poor wife in a
Georgia loony bin
she saw her children die
one by one
Thinking of his mother out
there in the backwater cemetery
her shroud faded
her eye sockets, windows for

spiders, "Bring them hands
from underneath those sheets so's
we can see them. Let us see what you
have beneath those sheets"
The sign on Charlie's door
"Making Love Is Good For You"
shot full of bulletholes

His brains liver and kidneys
gone up in smoke
"Making Love Is Good For You"
His stomach will hold no more
beans
no more bad coffee
his lips have seen their last
cigarette
O ain't it a shame what they did
To Charlie James. Have mercy ain't
it a shame.
They said his homicide was justified
the parrot D.A. "concurred"
The police were just doing their
duty, they said, and the
parrot D.A. "concurred, concurred"
O the parrot D.A. "concurred"
O ain't it a shame what they did

to poor Charlie James
"Making Love Is Good For You"
"Bring them hands from underneath
those sheets so's we can see them.
Let's see what you have beneath those
sheets."

Points of View

The pioneers and the indians
disagree about a lot of things
for example, the pioneer says that
when you meet a bear in the woods
you should yell at him and if that
doesn't work, you should fell him
The indians say that you should
whisper to him softly and call him by
loving nicknames
No one's bothered to ask the bear
what he thinks

Bitch

When's the last time you
saw a dog eat a dog

When men invented the term
Bitch
They were talking about
themselves

Datsun's Death

"Down in Puerto Rico, when
we didn't have no kerosene
we used the stuff to read by"
the stuff
he took his first drink
at twenty, and by the age of
40 had sauced up enough to fill
all the billboard bottles from
Lafitte's Galveston to Houston's
Texas
There's enough light in his belly
to fire all the gas lamps in
Cincinnati
He remembers getting burned in Cincinnati
his radiator was hot
his temperature was rising
like the white 68 Dodge grumbling
up Moeser Lane, as ferocious as a
pit-bull
The accident cop would later
say
It must have been built like a
tank
rammed into my piece of tail

a hit and run, you've been there
haven't you partner
haven't you?

It was A.T. and T. which reminded us
that the heaviest traffic occurs at
4:30 a.m.
All the phone circuits are busy
I loves you baby
You know i loves you baby!
Do you loves me baby?
I don't care what you women
say
Prometheus was a man
the X rays just came back
his liver looks terrible

For the ground crew
at the Kirksville
airport a sweetheart
is the otter jetstream
of Illinois Airlines
while the two-toned
Monte Carlo parked next
to the Robin breasted
cornfield is baby

For me heaven was
tooling around in the
driver's seat of my
280ZX
my honey of the midnight blue
my import car of the year
mutilated by the brazen chrome
of a snorting bull-car
hot and swerving under
the El Cerrito moon

Plymouth, Cadillac, Mercury
Montego, the automobile gods
rattled in their Richmond junkyards
Chrysler and Ford sales went down
30% the next day
And the shining new sacrifices on display
at banner-waving San Bruno
parking lots,
Wept from their windshields
Some used-up like my Datsun
Head mashed against the rhododendrons

On the Fourth of July in Sitka, 1982

On the fourth of July in Sitka
Filipinos sold shish-ka-bob from their
booths in the park
On the fourth of July in Sitka, the children
dressed in deerskin jackets
and coonskin caps
On the fourth of July in Sitka, you
could buy fishpie in the basement of St. Michael's
Church, where the vodka-drunken Russians used to
pray
But the red white and blue cake was not for sale

On the fourth of July in Sitka the people
kicked off shoes and ran through the
streets, pushing beds
On the fourth of July in Sitka, tour buses
with yellow snouts and square heads
delivered tourists to the Shee Atika lodge
where they stared at floats designed by
Sheldon Jackson College and
the Alaska Women in Timber
On the fourth of July in Sitka the
Gajaa Heen dancers performed, wearing their
Klan emblems of Beaver Wolf Killer Whale
Porpoise, and Dog Salmon

On the fourth of July in Sitka the Libertarian
Party announced the winners of its five dollar raffle
1st Prize, a Winchester .300 Magnum
2nd Prize, an Ithaca 12 gauge shotgun
3rd Prize, a Sportsman III knife

On the fourth of July in Sitka the
softball teams were honored at the American
Legion Club and the players drank champagne till dawn
On the fourth of July in Sitka, the night was
speckled with Japanese fireworks
sponsored by Alaska Lumber and Pulp

On the fifth of July in Sitka
a Canadian destroyer brought to Sitka
for the fourth of July in Sitka sailed
through Sitka Sound and out into the
Northern Pacific
All of the men on board stood at
attention, saluting their audience
three bald eagles, two ravens, and me
watching the whole show from Davidoff Hill
the fifth of July in Sitka

Petite Kid Everett

The bantamweight King of
Newark
He couldn't box
He couldn't dance
He just kept coming at
you, glass chin first
Taking five punches for
every one he connected with
you

Petite Kid Everett
He missed a lot
Slipped a lot and
By mid-life he'd
developed one heck
of a sorehead
Took to fighting in
the alley
Gave up wearing a mouthpiece
Beat up his trainers
Beat up the referee
Beat up his fans
Beat up everybody who was
in his corner

Even jumped on Houston Jr.
the lame pail boy
Who didn't have good sense
Petite Kid Everett
There's talk of a comeback
He's got new backers
He stands on one of the four
corners, near the Prudential Life
Building
Trading blows with ghosts
Don't it make you wanna cry?

Turning Pro

There are just so many years
you can play amateur baseball
without turning pro
All of a sudden you realize
you're ten years older than
everybody in the dugout
and that the shortstop could
be your son

The front office complains
about your slowness in making
the line-up
They send down memos about
your faulty bunts and point out
how the runners are always faking
you out
"His ability to steal bases
has faded" they say
They say they can't convince
the accountant that there's such
a thing as "Old Time's Sake"
But just as the scribes were
beginning to write you
off

as a has-been on his last leg
You pulled out that fateful
shut-out
and the whistles went off
and the fireworks scorched a
747
And your name lit up the scoreboard
and the fans carried you on their
shoulders right out of the stadium
and into the majors

Epistolary Monologue

My Dearest Michael:

My favorite lady-in-waiting is so loyal. She certainly can keep a secret. Every day at teatime she sneaks me three bottles of Beefeater. She knows that I can't stand tea. Today she brought me your note. This morning, she had to bring me two tablets of Myaatal. I still haven't recovered from my trip to America. Must have been the tacos and beans we ate at the Reagan's Ranch. That woman is so rude. You remember how she tried to upstage me during her trip to London? Wailing about town with her motorcycle escorts. Got up in that tacky red dress and those wide-brimmed hats that make her resemble a witch. I was speaking to her husband, and the poor man fell asleep. Still telling the same jokes.

But back to your note, my sweet. Michael, I was so touched, but how would it look if another scandal happened to the Windsors? They still haven't gotten over Uncle Edward. If I ran away with you, the public would take away our allowances and evict us from Buckingham Palace. How would we survive? On hotdogs and beans. Our only experience is shaking hands and smiling. And there doesn't seem to be an awful demand for people who know how to walk in processions.

Somebody has to keep a level head. Andrew carrying on with that tart. Diana locked up in her room starving herself, all because she found out Charles's secret. The secret we've kept from the public all these years. Her look-alike is threatening to reveal the whole sordid business if she doesn't receive more money. And Princess Anne. Granted that she is my daughter, but sometimes I think that she's so ugly she should be arrested for public ugliness. The poor young man she's living with is always talking about leaving her. He says that he has to put a bag over her head in order to get a good night's sleep. So please understand, my darling. I do love you. Queens have feelings too, but if I married you, a poor laborer, who would feed my horses and my dogs?

Well, it's 2:00 a.m. here in the Palace. As the Americans say, "I'm in my gin." I just turned off all of the lights. Everyone here is so wasteful. Philip and my bodyguards are in the next room watching videocassettes of *Dynasty* and squealing with delight. O, I wish I could be like that Krystle. Always taking chances, going where her heart leads. But I've grown accustomed to my duty, my position, and the grand tradition of which I am a symbol.

And so, don't be cross with me when my lady-in-waiting delivers this note to you. Goodbye, my darling. And please forgive me for having you arrested. But when we were lying in bed that morning, and you complained about what you would and wouldn't do, I had to put you in your place. Though we were lovers, I was still your sovereign, which meant that my wish was your command.

Love,
Lilibet

Monkey Island

To the monkeys on Monkey Island
the danger signal for man is the
same as that for an approaching
python
That's why the monkeys on Monkey
Island chatter their tails off
when we stand in front of their
cages
They know something that we
Zoo Keepers don't know
Haven't you thought of a person
and said to yourself
that snake

The Pope Replies to the Ayatollah Khomeini

My Dear Khomeini:

I read your fourteen thousand dollar
ad asking me why the Vatican waited
all of these years to send an envoy
to complain about conditions in Iran
You're right, we should have sent one
when the Shah was in power, look,
I'm in total agreement with you
Khomeini, that Christ, had he lived in
Iran under the Shah, would have led the
biggest damned revolt you ever saw

Believe me, Khomeini, I knew about
the Shah's decadence, his extravagance
his misdeeds, and how he lolled about
in luxury with Iran's loot
I knew about the trail of jewels which
led to his Dad's capture
but a fella has to eat and so when
David Rockefeller asked me to do something
how could I refuse?

You can afford to be holier than thou

What is it, 30 dollars per barrel these days?
You must be bathing in oil
While each day I suffer a new indignity

You know that rock record they made me
do? It's 300 on the Charts which is about
as low as you can get.
And I guess you read where I
had to call in all those Cardinals and
for the first time reveal the Vatican
budget?
I had to just about get down on my hands
and knees to get them to co-sign for a
loan
The Vatican jet has a mechanical problem
and the Rolls-Royce needs a new engine
The staff hasn't been paid in months
and the power company is threatening to
turn off the candles
To add to that, the building inspector
has listed us as having 30,000 code
violations
I'm telling you, Khomeini, that
so many people are leaving the church
I have this nightmare where I

wake up one day in Los Angeles and
I'm the only one left

Pretty soon we'll be one of those
cults you read about in the *San
Francisco Chronicle*
And so, Khomeini, I promise
you that when we pay off the
deficit, I won't send an envoy
I'll come visit you myself

I'd like to discuss this plan
that Patriarch Dimitrios, of
the Greek Orthodox Church, and I
just came up with

You know, we haven't spoken to
those fellows in 900 years but
when you are 20 million dollars
in the red
You'll talk to anybody

Inaugural Day, 1981

I feel like a Zulu
spying from a rock while
below, the settlers exchange
toasts on the grounds where
a massacre of the Zulus occurred
They are filthy rich
Their wives are dolled-up in
black mink
There is much hugging and
squealing
These people like
Glenn Miller a whole lot
   52 of their countrymen
have been freed by the barbarians
overseas
   "Just out of the trees. The
Only way I'm going back is in a
B-52," he said, putting some hair
on his chest, and passing around
a jug of whiskey
   The settlers shoot at stars
   The settlers jitterbug all
   night
On the Zulu grounds
I have nine children buried there
nine were all they could find

Mossy

If you want to save some money
Always stare a gift cat in the mouth
Especially if you bought him on
Russian Hill
He might have developed
A palate

Untitled

When California is split in two
The Northern part will be called
The Republic of Jambalaya
The Southern part will be called
Summer Camp

Grizzly

He always prided himself on
never being caught with his paws down
The flying grizzly left his bear
tracks at fifty thousand feet
his life, a daily peach blossom
He always managed to find some
hot honey to dip into
He was smiling all the time
Licking his lips, till Mrs.
Grizzly discovered him in the
bush with some outside trim of
a wonderful red cabbage and Mrs.
Grizzly grounded her
Teddy Bear
the rough rider under her fur coat
she was not taken in by his sweet
word-bees
Last trip back to the cave
he felt like he'd entered customs
after a return from an enemy city
What are these claw marks doing on your back?
Are those huckleberry stains on the front
of your pants?

Why do you have that fishy smell?
The divorce left him belly-up

He's somewhere right now
dressed in white and black
checkered pants
being led at the neck by a rope
While he bangs on a dirty
bass drum
a little monkey toots a whistle
and little dogs taunt him
and little children tug at
his ears

Judas

Funny about best friends
huh, Lord
Always up in your face
laughing and talking
leading the praise after
your miracles
That Judas, you had great
hopes for him
Good background
Good-looking, even in a
corduroy suit, made in
Poland, and thirty dollar
shoes
It was his quiet appeal that
kept the group in wine money

As soon as you turned your
back, he took your business
to the Goyim
Told them you going around
telling everybody you the
son-of-god
See how careful you have to

be about whom you go bar-
hopping with, Jesus

Now you're drowsy, Jesus
They've pricked you full of
Thorazine
They've given you electro-
convulsive therapy
You don't know where you
are
You have sores where the
straight-jacket doesn't fit
You're wringing wet from
where you've been sweatin
all night
You squirm on filthy straw

But stick it out, Jesus
where you're going
the drums don't stop
They serve Napa Valley
champagne at every meal
Everybody smokes big cigars
Sweet Angel hair be tingling
your back while you invent
proverbs in a hot tub

Where Judas is going
the people don't know how
to fix ribs
the biscuits taste like
baking soda
The wine is sweet and sticky
Flowers can't grow on this
landscape of jinxed hearts
the Field of Blood
to this day it's called
the Field of Blood

Dialog Outside the Lakeside Grocery

The grocery had provided him with
boxes of rotten lettuce
He was loading them onto a
yellow pick-up truck
He was a frail white man and
wore a plaid woolen shirt and
frayed dungarees
I was sitting in a gray chevrolet
rent-a-dent
"I have eight adult geese and
twenty-six ducks," he said
and I said
"I'll bet you have a big management
problem," and he said
"They're no trouble at all. My
wife raised two of them in the house.
When she goes near their pen
the geese waddle towards her
and nibble the lettuce out of her
hand"
"I'd never think of killing them"
he said
"They keep me out of the bars"

Invasion

Tough guy
He fondles the public
as though it were a
kissing baby
Playing giddyup with his
Stetson
His wife has this thing about
the color blue
Why is it that when the old
men have power the young men
fly home in star-spangled skins

Beats me
The liars on t.v.
They have turned me against the
head of hair, parted on the left side
Under the eyes of god, at night
They cry into sympathetic bourbon
Casper, the malevolent duppy
Doesn't crack a smile in his
hard pinched face
They bombed the mad house by
accident
A level headed pilot came back

Three times, the nurse testified
"I'll remember his grin for the
rest of my life."

The mad house is located on the
Island of Grenada
It is where they chain the crazy
people

Untitled

Alaska's rape
dismemberment
disassembled piece by piece
and shipped to the lower
forty-eight so that people
in Dallas may own whale-
sized Cadillacs and lear
jets which cost Alaska an
arm and a leg just like
ravished Jamaica whose
stolen sugar built Mansfield
Park where idle gang rapers
discuss flower beds and
old furniture
Jamaica, Alaska, sisters
dragged into an alley
used and abandoned

Poem for Two Daughters

Everybody wants to know
Where's your oldest daughter
Her first sentence was
phenomenon
Sixteen years later she
stands before you, drawing
on a cigarette
She says she's found you
out
She has exactly eighty dollars
to her name
she thinks she grown
She says she wants her emancipation
You tell her to spell it
She calls you a nerd, a dork
and other words you hear on the
3:15 Arlington #7 Bus
The Yo-Yo special

We used to chide the sightseeing
middle aged in those days when
we stood on our heads outside the Dom
Now, we are the ones sitting on the
greyline

We cannot figure out what it is
we are staring at

Our stomachs hurt
We gaze from houses with un-
obstructed views of the Bay
thirty years ago we couldn't come
up here
Nowadays the neighbors bring pies
Our daughters are either standing up
for the first time or flying

The youngest one puts everything
into her mouth, pencils, your hair
graham crackers, the cat, the car keys
even the Sesame Street book covered
with blue-fuzzed creatures with
purple noses and egg-shaped eyes
She trounces the trampoline in
the kindergym but's too plump for
the Olympics
Her first sentence was: "I see"

The oldest one, as fast as
Clifford Brown on Cherokee
Of another system, impatient

with your inability to cope with
the basic concepts of her world
grinds you up with her mind
Intellectually shoves you about
like you the
wildest Turkey in the state of
Georgia, guiding the hunters to
your roost
You have to fall back on
"It's so because I say it's so"

The differences between the three
would be revealed if someone were to
ask each what they would do if
the world was offered to them on
a silver platter
The youngest one would say
I'd eat it
or at least jump up and down
on it a few times
The oldest one would strut up and down
in front of the world, scolding the world
about its ancient corruption
She'd fast
By the time the question reached
you
the world would have run out of
bones

Phoebe

Phoebe is the 9th satellite
of Saturn
Phoebe is the moon
bending the golden blades
of El Cerrito
A voice brighter than the
lights of the harness racing
fields
Snow has returned to the Sierras
snow has returned to the Rockies
Mount Shasta of opium-
headed Lemurian ceremony
Altars made of whalebone
five thousand years old
California tumbled into the
Pacific
The Indians wrote:
I am burning for snow
said Mount Diablo

Once, because I missed
the snow I made a yellow
streak to Montpelier, Vermont
to witness a white rainbow

to entwist myself in a white rainbow
my Montpelier, population one
she used to belong to a
fisherman

Untitled

I know of a man who treated his body like a dog

the dog ran away

The Middle Class Blues

MONOLOGUE

I can't believe it's 1994. Back in 84 it meant something, but nowadays being middle class and a nickel won't buy you a cup of coffee. During the rest of the 80s the frig was still full and you could always mambo in Guadalajara during the discount off seasons. But by the beginning of the 90s, the only difference between us and the poor was that everything they owned was on their backs while everything we owned was being lent to us by the banks. The banks were on our backs. I was over my head in billy dues. Me and the Mrs. argued so about money that one day she just upped and left. And these were supposed to be our golden years. Some golden years. I can't seem to save over a couple of hundred dollars and I'm spending a third more than I'm making. It's only a matter of time before I have to visit one of those bankruptcy consultants. Talking about the new poor. Never thought it would happen to me. What happened to the old poor? I dunno. They were kicked out of the bus stations, the parks and the welfare hotels a long time ago. Some say they went South. Others say that the society people had them shipped to Central America because down there they know how to handle the poor. Wherever they are, they must have been desperate. They left behind their blues. I'm lucky I guess. I can still afford a martini.

I

I got the middle class blues
I play by middle class rules
O, this middle class life
Is a life full of strife
The bourgeois state can be
A sweet and sour pill
When the first rolls around
You gotta deal with the bills

So hey, Mr. Bartender,
Bring me a dry vermouth and gin
Fix me a black olive and a big martini
Before I hit the wind

II

I constantly get headaches
And my back is often sore
Being the first one on the freeway
Is becoming such a chore
At work they got a robot
That soon will have my job
I'm too old to start all over
Too old to learn to rob

So hey, Mr. Bartender
Bring me a dry vermouth and gin

Fix me a black olive and a big martini
Before I hit the wind

III
The roof is always leaking
The plumbing needs some screws
Everybody on the block, it seems
Knows how to bar-b-cue
My next door neighbors are ticked at me
My lawn is turning brown
There's always something that must be fixed
Everytime you turn around

Hey, hey, Mr. Bartender
Bring me a dry vermouth and gin
Fix me a black olive and a big martini
Before I hit the wind

IV
My son is getting married
To a woman older than me
He just turned twenty the other
week
She's going on sixty-three
My daughter's on narcotics
Her eyes are always red

The car wouldn't start this morning
And I toss and turn in bed

So hey, Mr. Bartender
Bring me a dry vermouth and gin
Fix me a black olive and a big martini
Before I hit the wind

V
The communists say I'm an ingrate
The capitalists took my house
The old people say I neglect them
The young call me a louse
The tax man sent me a letter
He's coming here tonight
Sometimes it gets so heavy
At home, I'm never right

So hey, Mr. Bartender
Bring me a dry vermouth and gin
Fix me a black olive and a big martini
Before I hit the wind

VI
The Doctor says it's no good
To have this stress and mess

The ulcers that will get you
A classy middle class nest
A cat that won't eat store food
Must have its abalone
And don't forget the deadline
To pay the alimony

So hey, Mr. Bartender
Bring me a dry vermouth and gin
Fix me a black olive and a big martini
Before I hit the wind

VII
Well, I'm tired of paying the dentist
And going under the knife
And doing all the things you do
To stay the bourgeois life
The rich they live in heaven
The poor they live in hell
And I live somewhere in between
A sign outside says for sale

So hey, Mr. Bartender
Bring me a dry vermouth and gin
Fix me a black olive and a big martini
Let me go on get this wind

Oakland Blues

Well it's six o'clock in Oakland
and the sun is full of wine
I say, it's six o'clock in Oakland
and the sun is red with wine
We buried you this morning, baby
in the shadow of a vine

Well, they told you of the sickness
almost eighteen months ago
Yes, they told you of the sickness
almost eighteen months ago
You went down fighting, daddy. Yes
You fought Death toe to toe

O, the egrets fly over Lake Merritt
and the blackbirds roost in trees
O, the egrets fly over Lake Merritt
and the blackbirds roost in trees
Without you little papa
what O, what will become of me

O, it's hard to come home, baby
To a house that's still and stark
O, it's hard to come home, baby

To a house that's still and stark
All I hear is myself
thinking
and footsteps in the dark

Martine's Keen Eyes

"I take them with me to the fights
every night," Martine says
On the top floor of the Chelsea
In a two room, one kitchen apartment
with white walls, Martine lives with
Elvin Jones records and *Paris Match*
and wall to wall boxers, staring out
at you from the blacks and whites of
Marline's keen eyes, and the people
stop by, to tell her how much they
love her pictures, and how they moved
them so: The curly gray-haired black
woman who wanders about New York in a
rent hospital gown, her only friend
a milk-stained overcoat.
The gang members with Creole faces,
smiling, in front of a Chevrolet, all
but one, dead within six months
wax-faced in Puerto Rican coffins
bussed by comrades; the sassy
bathing-suited little black girl who
charmed an adoring fire hydrant into
spouting her a lake; the pint-sized
dynamite who spars in front of Martine's

mirrors for hours at a time, and the
Inca-faced four year old who never lost
a fight, in the clubs smelling of pizza
and hotdogs where the fight people drink
beer for hours in the fight clubs
watching the fights

St. Louis Woman

He loves to see that orbed heat collapse behind the white
Jefferson arc as the downtown St. Louis sun temples burst
Orange as the inside of a Balaban's lobster they cater in
the room of Renoirish Third Reich Speer-room nude por-
traits where Wash. U. grad student waiters resemble the t.v.
crew filming a restaurant scene in *As the World Turns*. On a
stool outside a black man in little boy's cap and white
butcher's coat attracts customers with the gleaming stars of
his gold teeth. For four days a storebought apricotheaded
St. Louis woman in poor white powder and tobacco-road
mascaraed eyelashes told the other waitresses in the Forest
Park Hotel to quit putting cream and sugar in his coffee
because "He looks spoiled. Big and spoiled."

Daughters of Davy Crockett and Dan Boone with high-
Cherokee cheekbones, St. Louis women call closeted planta-
tions with monopoly-board street names, "home" behind fake
second empire gates which are locked at night to keep out
the townies, riding bicycles, their eyes buried in the streets,
the only blacks wear supermarket names on their t-shirts

They stand on the street's dividing line selling rush
hour copies of the *St. Louis Post Dispatch* like the apple-
capped Irish lads in a book about the life and times of Jacob
Riis

They are the last people in the nation who take out
their billfolds to show you their relatives and their girl-
friends' and boyfriends' relatives and that time they went to
Atlantic City

St. Louis is surrounded by ninety municipalities. Only a Filipino with a Harvard M.A. in business can untangle the town, Emile said. Emile said that St. Louis women are dumb blondes who stand you up. Equal rights to them means the right to tantalize but not to put out, Emile said.

"Are you Bruce Lee?" they asked Emile when he landed in Harlem.

Feeling tomorrow and twenty-two, a St. Louis woman told him she could run a whole radio station. She knew where you could fetch a Gucci raincoat for one hundred dollars. In her poetry she is "a black rose." He told her that if her skin really needed a flower why not an African violet to go with her yellow eyes. He told her that her eyes were all the evidence we needed to prove that ancient Asiatics reached Madagascar. He told her that a black rose was common and that she was anything but common and that she was as rare as a white tiger rarely seen in the jungles of India or rare as the image of a white owl carrying off a white ermine in the Bird Book we saw in the museum off Big Bend where we learned that the first words said on the telephone constituted a cry for help.

In the Steinberg auditorium he asked the Dalai Lama's stand in why there were black gods with nigger minstrel white lips and great Nigerian mound noses in Nepalese paintings dated 3,000 B.C.

Before rushing to the next question he said they represented Time. He told the "black rose" that she was as rare as Time hung on a monastery wall, while outside buddhists blow conch horns and chant like a chorus of frogs.

St. Louis women are rabbit-furred hookers who hustle to star wars in the steeple chase room of the chase park hotel where Gorgeous George dressed in sequined Evel Knievel jumpsuit discos to Elvis Presley and the hogged-necked bouncers in blazers threaten to break your arm. There are portraits in that room of horses, skins shining like chestnuts, life-sized statues of jockeys in polka-dotted blouses. The lamps are shaped like racing horns.

St. Louis women write body poetry, play the harp for the symphony and take up archery.

St. Louis women wash cook and clean for St. Louis women who write body poetry, play the harp for the symphony, and take up archery.

A St. Louis woman is the automatic writing hand for a spirit named Ida Mae of the red dress cult who rises from the Mississippi each night to check out the saloons before last call.

She rises from the big river G. Redmond calls Black River, Mike Castro's River Styx, and every body knows about Muddy Waters; St. Louis women are daughters of Episcopalian ministers who couldn't sit still for Grant Wood

Sternly scarfed they stare straight ahead inside Doberman Pinscher station wagons. Their husbands work for McDonnell Douglas, Ralston Purina, and Anheuser-Busch.

(They still talk about how old man Busch was so rich that when his son killed a man it was the trial judge who served time)

The great grandfather of a St. Louis woman appears in the 100 years of lynching horror book because he owned 300 acres and white men wanted those acres

The grandmother of a St. Louis woman told her that no man can say "I Love You" like a black man. "Velvet be dripping from his lips," a unique experience like the one recounted by a man in the bar of the St. Louis airport about the time when Nanette Fabray came into the audience and sat on his lap, New Year's Eve, The Mark Hopkins Hotel, San Francisco

On Sunday he stuffed the frig with dungeness crabs

You can find the quilts of St. Louis women patched with real chipmunks and birds in the Jefferson museum next to the Lindbergh collection "Nothing like flying across the Atlantic in a one-seater" he said, "When she rocks, you rock, when you thrust so does she, and when she dives it's as if your soul bought the circus and you owned all the ferris wheels, *The Spirit of St. Louis!*"

A black man wrote a song about a St. Louis woman that go Hello Central, give me five o'nine, hello central give me five o' nine, the St. Louis woman said she liked my line about a man entering a woman's love pond, she thought i said love mine.

like a Mississippi school boy loves his mint and rye i love to see that evening sun go down when the St. Louis women come calling around

Many St. Louis women are from Kansas City

The year was 1914

W. C. Handy wrote a ragtime march with a blues
tango introduction (The Tango, derived from
the African Tangenda, was once banned all the
way down to the Argentinian South Pole)
but there was something missing.
"What this music needs is a Vamp," the trombonist
said, and that's how "St. Louis Woman" came into
being
The big publishers wouldn't chance her
They were only interested in Whiteman's blues
and so, at the age of 40, W. C. Handy went to
bat for his Vamp, publishing 10,000
copies of "St. Louis Blues" at his own expense

Handy flew up the Fatty Grimes diamond
from Memphis and presented it to her
(Hippolite's "Mystical Marriage")
He chauffeured her across the nation in
a whale-length white cadillac like the
one i once saw Bob Hope get out of
He introduced her to a Carnegie Hall
sell-out audience which she delighted
with her shanty-town ways
Sometimes she was as icy as the Portage glacier
in Portage, Alaska,
at other times she was tropical as the

Miami airport at 5:30 when the Santeria
jets sweep in

Resting under that mellow Creole
river in a silver satin slip
the color of an enshrined coronet
mooning on the silky meat of a giant
clam
guarded by chocolate dandies
Irises on their creamy waistcoats
and a Tennessee billygoat covered with
cowrie shells
St. Louis Woman

Bitter Chocolate

I
Only the red-skins know what
I know, and they ain't talkin
So I keep good friends with
turkey whiskey
Or try to do some walkin
Don't want no lovin
Ain't anxious to play
And you want to know how
I got that way
Bitter Chocolate
Bitter Chocolate
Blood like ice water
Kisses taste like snuff
Why are all of my women
so jive and full of stuff

They call me a runaway father
But they won't give me no job
They say I'm a thief
when I'm the one gettin
robbed
Most of me was missing when
They brought me back from

Nam
My mama and my sister
cried for me
But my government didn't give
a damn
Bitter Chocolate
Bitter Chocolate
Sullied and sullen black
man

II
When they come to lynch somebody
Always breaking down my door
When they lay somebody off
I'm the first one off the floor
Bitter Chocolate
Bitter Chocolate
Veins full of brine
Skin sweatin turpentine
Cold and unfriendly
Got ways like a lizard

III
Well, it's winter in Chicago on
a February day
O'Hare airport is empty and

I call you on the line
It's 9:00 A.M. where you are
and the phone rings seven times
Hello, who is this? you say
in a sleeping heaving sigh
Your woman in the background yells
Who in the hell is that guy
Bitter Chocolate
Bitter Chocolate
I'm standing in the rain
All my love is all squeezed
out
All that I can give is pain
All that I can give is pain

The Smiley School

July 2, 1982—Juneau. Today the Rotterdam is in port. "We don't make any money from tourists," Andy says. "They just come into town, buy trinkets, and return to their ship." Randall Ackley is driving me to the Lemon Creek jail, where I instruct my class of two: Cornboy and Sanchez. Cornboy writes about the town in Iowa, where people drive tractors on the highway and wear levi shorts. "The midwestern maize grows as tall as a basketball player," Cornboy says. Cornboy says he knows more about the Eagle Dance than the Indians.

Sanchez writes about Nam. His lines crackle and ignite as though they were participants in a literary firefight. They bite like the pesky snake the Ghanians called "Dead Yesterday," it was so quick. His invective is as violent as the black G.I. he told us about, who splattered the mess hall walls with officers' brains. "I dunno, he just went berserk. Docile one minute, like a park deer, next minute, a mad minute."

In the lower forty-eight, the jails are filled with blacks. Mexican Americans, Puerto Ricans, Cubans and Indians. Up here in Lemon Creek it's Eskimos and Indians.

Randall's Swedish grandmother lives in Sweden. For her, the Italians, French, and British are black people. The Irish, descendants of a crew whose fishing boat wandered too far from the coast of North Africa. Like the Smiley family. The Smileys were part Indian and part black. They didn't want to go to the black school, and they didn't want to go to the Indian school and so down in North Carolina there's a white school, a black school, and a Smiley school.

July 1st 1982

What do you do in a town where
11:00 p.m. looks like noon
and the streets are deserted
What do you do in a town
where space is so tight that
people build houses on boggy ground
or beneath avalanche-prone mountains
covered with Holstein hides
Suicide the therapist said at
Auke Lake
There's suicide up here
knifings in bars
Alcoholism
Up here it's like the
war without the sound effects
In the Viet Nam War
58,000 Americans died by homicide
59,000 Americans died by suicide

Ice Age

Like a gargantuan tongue, coated blue from the millions of tons of pressure, a man decapitating ice monster, calving upon those who defy it the Mendenhall Glacier glowers at visitors from where it lies, pouring forth into a sapphire colored pool, at Tongass National Forest. Two tipsy soldiers, intoxicated from Ranier Ale (green death) wandered too close to it and were "eaten." Like all of Veil's creatures, it contracts in anger from the teenaged jeers, and beer cans, lying upon its great white royal coat, extending backwards to hundreds of miles

The glacialist warned them. The young glacialist said that all of Veil's creatures demand respect, but the City Elders laughed at the glacier's impudence and the glacialist's hippie clothes

On the last day of Juneau the sky was as blue as a Harlem Monday. Small planes squatted upon the water like mosquitoes, Alaska's state bird

A ship, the Royal Viking, reposed majestically in the port as its baby boats ferried people into the city

At Dingby Dave's the folks were enjoying the clam chowder that was hot from start to finish

Exiled New Englanders were trying out their new indoor tennis courts, and transplanted Californians were in the sauna

People were chatting and tasting smoked salmon behind Robert's Mountain

The guys and gals were hoisting a few in the Red Dog
Saloon

Cars were lined up for a half-mile as passengers
awaited their turn at

mining for McNuggets at the new McDonald's

In the House of Wickersham tourists were sampling
the flaming sourdough and a mother spanked her son for
tinkering with the Chickering grand piano, the one that
Judge Wickersham brought from Baranof castle in Sitka.
Inside the Lemon Creek jail, the prisoners were having a
potlatch supper of muk tuk seal fat seal oil herring eggs
smoked salmon and halibut cheeks

The congregation of the Russian Orthodox Church was
split down the middle

Some wanted to remain loyal to Moscow, others
wanted independence (the Catholic Bishop for the area
dresses like a lumberjack)

All at once, the sky grew as white as Alaska Cotton

as the Mendenhall Glacier fired its frozen chunks upon

the town

The only exit from Juneau is by air

but nobody would be flying that day

The Bears prayed to the Bear God

the mountain goats climbed higher

and from his shack in the mountains

the glacialist's eyes followed the

Mendenhall Glacier as it

crept towards Canada

But Nobody Was There

I heard a crying child in the other room
I entered the room, but nobody was there
I heard a spider crawl across the silverware
I opened the drawer, but nobody was there
I heard your steps creeping up the stairs
I opened the door, but nobody was there
But nobody was there, but nobody, but nobody
But nobody was there

I saw your spirit sitting in a chair
I turned my head, but nobody was there
I heard a knock and the doorknob turned
I answered the door, but nobody was there
I saw my love in her funeral bier
I turned on the lights, but nobody was there
But nobody was there, but nobody, but nobody
But nobody was there

I heard your laughter on the summer's air
I called your name, but nobody was there
I saw you bare, riding your favorite black mare
I ran to the woods, but nobody was there
I saw you by the moon, you were combing your

hair, I rushed outside, but nobody was there
But nobody was there, but nobody, but nobody
But nobody was there

Slaveship, German Model

I
A pout is a thing with scales
Even when gliding across a marble
floor and tailored by Adolfo
I am in a room of pouts
the clothes they wear would set me
back three months rent
 Off camera, he displays a mink ring
 On camera, he talks about his
 "disenfranchisement
 his oppression"; a word that once
had its hand out has gone and gotten
a manicurist

II
He said that he bought a Mercedes
because the holes on the side
reminded him of a slaveship

At the entrance to J.F.K.
there should be a sign:
"Welcome to New York
a rhetoric delicatessen"

Lake Bud

Lake Merritt is Bud Powell's piano
The sun tingles its waters
Snuff-jawed pelicans descend
tumbling over each other like
Bud's hands playing Tea For Two
or Two For Tea

Big Mac Containers, tortilla chip, Baby Ruth
wrappers, bloated dead cats, milkshake
cups, and automobile tires
float on its surface
Seeing Lake Merritt this way is
like being unable to hear
Bud Powell at Birdland
Because people are talking
Clinking glasses of whiskey and
shouting
"Hey, waiter"

Home Sweet Earth

Home Sweet Earth
Home Sweet Earth
Our first class berth in space
Stomping ground of the human race
Designer of Dorothy Dandridge's face
Of Siamese cats, and Max Roach sets
Of beaches, incredibly sandy
Home Sweet Earth
Home Sweet Earth
Your waters are chicken soup
To our souls
You give us goldenrod and
Breakfast rolls
Italian spaghetti and Dizzy
Gillespie
Zimbabwe, and Lady Day
Home Sweet Earth
Home Sweet Earth
Thank you for French Fries
and Creme de Menthe
For Rock and Roll
For the Super Bowl
For scallops and the Alps
For George Clinton's funk
For Thelonius Monk

For Trumpets and trombones
For the Cathedral of Cologne
For Ka.Bah's black stone
Home Sweet Earth
Home Sweet Earth
Mother of legba and Damballah
Of kinky haired Jesus
Of Muhammed and Gautama
Of Confucius, and Krishna
Of Siva and Vishnu
Home Sweet Earth
Home Sweet Earth
May you be shamrock green again
May you stay out of the way of
Black holes
May you spin forever without
End
May you survive the nuclear deals
May you survive the chemical spills
May you survive the bio-technology
May you survive the peckerwood theology
May the Big Crunch theory be all wet!
May you survive man
May you survive man
Home Sweet Earth
Home Sweet Earth
You give us something to stand on

I'm Running For The Office Of Love

I'm running for the office of love
My heart is in the ring
I'm bad at making speeches
So I guess I'll have to sing
A tune of moons and flowers
And things that go with Spring
And things that go with Spring

Love is so political
I don't remember it this way
They'll curse you if you play it straight
And kill you if you're gay
They say that love is dangerous
That it's best to do without
So somebody has to speak for love
That's why I'm singing out

I'm running for the office of love
My heart is in the ring
I'm bad at making speeches
So I guess I'll have to sing
A tune of moons and flowers
And things that go with Spring
And things that go with Spring

Love is like a loaded gun
A fool stands in its way
There was one man who was on the run
He was trying to get away
But love took careful aim at him
She brought him in her sights
He bought her wine and perfume
And all her favorite delights
He hadn't been paying attention
And given love her due
She took away his peace of mind
And plagued him with the blues

I'm running for the office of love
My heart is in the ring
I'm bad at making speeches
So I guess I'll have to sing
A tune of moons and flowers
And things that go with Spring
And things that go with Spring

They say that love is dangerous
It's on the radio
That holding hands is fatal
A kiss can bring you low
The papers they keep shouting

That "LOVE MEANS DOOM AND GLOOM"
So love is lying low for awhile
Until her next big bloom
Until her next big bloom

I'm running for the office of love
My heart is in the ring
I'm bad at making speeches
So I guess I'll have to sing
A tune of moons and flowers
And things that go with Spring
And things that go with Spring

Life Is A Screwball Comedy

Life is a screwball comedy
life is a screwball comedy
It's Gary Grant leaning too
far back in a chair
It's Bill Cosby with a
nose full of hair
It's Richard Pryor
with his heart on fire
Life is a screwball comedy
life is a screwball comedy
It's Moms Mabley leaving her
dentures home
It's the adventures of Hope and Bing
It's Bert Williams doin' a buck and wing
It's Stepin Fetchit sauntering before
a mule
It's matches in your shoes
It's April Fool
Life is a screwball comedy
Life is a screwball comedy
It's Scatman Crothers with his
sexy grin
It's W. C. Fields with a bottle
of gin

It's Maggie gettin' in her digs
at Jiggs
It's Desi and Lucy having a doozy
of a fight
It's Pigmeat Martin and Slappy White
Life is a Screwball Comedy
Life is a Screwball Comedy
It's Will Rogers twirling a rope
It's Buster Keaton wearing his
famous mope
It's Fatty Arbuckle in a leaking
boat
It's a scared rabbit
And a tricky Coyote
Life is a screwball comedy
Life is a screwball comedy
It's Eddie Murphy's howl
It's Whoopie Goldberg's stroll
It's Fred Allen's jowls
Its Pee-Wee Herman's clothes
It's Hardy giving Laurel a hard time
It's Chaplin up on his toes
Life is a screwball comedy
life is a screwball comedy
life is a screwball comedy
And the joke's on us

New Verse, 1989–2006

Nov 22, 1988

In California
The day looks as though it's seen a ghost
An obstreperous storm is heading for the Sierras
The forecast is "cloudy gloomy and gray"
There is not a dry eye on TV,
They're showing the archival footage
Air Force One setting down in Dallas
The bouquet in Jackie's hands
The cruel scene in Washington as
Politicians grapple with your coffin
The riderless horse,
Little John John saluting
The face down in Cuba
Ich bin Ein Berliner

You told the White Citizens
Councils that if you could
Negotiate with Khrushchev then they could
Negotiate with Negroes
You made old Miss
Swallow hard
You slammed Alabam'
Stuffing its throat with
Jim Crow

Even on Dan Rather's face,

There is a struggle

It's been twenty years and

His youngest wants to know

Why did they murder you?

The theories are as common as homeless

People, huddled together in

The Port Authority

Under a bridge in Santa Cruz

Lafayette Park

Across the street from the White House

He agrees with the day

He feels like an old back pain

Eloisa wants to know, why

He is acting like a grinch

As he swivels, grumpily,

In her barber's chair

And maybe Carla is right when she says

You were like all the rest—only smoother

But when they took you out, Jack

It was as though

His generation was hit

In the belly with a medicine ball

They never fully recovered

Their wind
Their shape
Their tone and
They don't care what the
Tabloids say, Jack
You are still their boy

And maybe it's best that you
Left them, waving from a motorcade
A smile bigger than Texas
Fresh as that Oct. day Askia and he
Saw you stride into the Carlyle Hotel
Bareheaded, unovercoated
Surrounded by men
Shaking in their long johns
It's not pretty what's become of US
It's like the room inside a grisly
Crime movie, about which the homicide
detective warns
"Don't go in there"
It smells like something
That's been dead in the sun
Too long
It jerks about like the new chief's syntax

It has the style of an inside

Trader's ill-fitting collar
It bungles along like
Your lunkish successors
In black tie, and tails, executing a mean
Fox Trot at the Inaugural
Ball

May Day, 1989

At one time
People would quake when faced with
Your crooked smirk
Except the chairman
Who thought that you were
Ridiculing the birthmark
lying on his crown
like a purple Florida

Who does he think he is
Why you and Comrade Joe and
Comrade Molotov used to stand
In your goodwill overcoats at
The May Day parades
Eyeing those cheerleader's thighs
As you guzzled Stoli vodka
Of the Czars

But now, on the other side of fifty
Without your glasses
You can't tell the difference between a
3 and an 8
It takes a long time for you to pee
This morning you forgot where you
Parked your car

The only drama in your life is
When the Doctor says,
"The tests came back negative"

He says you have to give up
Chocolates, pancakes
And limit your breakfast
To Wheat Bran, as thrilling
As a lecture on Dialectics
As exciting as a meeting of
The Politbureau

The young ones don't know
With their Calvin Kleins and
Jackson moonwalks
That you and your generation
Shivered like the strings of
Shostakovich in the winter of
4I, as earnest fascists invaded
The motherland
Wearing those movie helmets
That concealed their eyes
Vowing to skin Moscow alive

These kids think that
Sacrifice means

A U2 concert
Was canceled
Or going without Pepsi

They couldn't care Mickey Mouse
About Zhukov, Malinovsky, and
Chernyakovsky, who earned their
Epaulets at Moscow, Stalingrad
And Kursk during Generalissimo Winter
Who blew the Nazi army away

These kids
They trip over the words of
The Internationale
The chairman's wife dresses like
Ivana Trump
And agents from Holiday
Inn are giving Red Square the
Once over
There's even talk of burying Lenin
And the Kremlin elevator
Operator knows more than you
"You still here?" he asked you
Yesterday morning,
One of those Sony Walkman's
Pinned to his ears

You had to read about it
In Pravda, which
Soon, no doubt, will
Include a comics section

"Today Andrei Gromyko
retired from the Central
Committee"
The American Press
will call you deadwood
A hack, a burr in the side
Of Perestroika

It's sad what happens
To old revolutionaries
Whose salad days have peaked

While everybody else is
Downtown having a party
You're sitting in the park
Feeding sparrows
Who don't know theory
From bread crumbs

Open Heart
for C.B.

True love is
When you lose ten pounds
He loses five
On the day they cut you
He couldn't eat

True love is
Your idle Fox car
And your fickle garrulous cat
Looking as though they haven't
A friend in the world

True love is
Your daughter and your
Husband holding you up
You're taking your post-
Operative steps
The infusion pump
"IMED 980"
Is leading the way
They pretend that
You're the queen and
It's Parliament's first day

True love is
You lying in bed
Tubes sprouting from you
Like the orchid stems on
Your night table
You are as vulnerable
As the flowers that Nancy
Sent
The note attached said
"Water Immediately!"

True love is
Your husband watching
The color return to your face
The radio is tuned to Monterey
The nurses say that they can't
Locate your veins, but he manages
To find your fragile hand
He's listening to A. Hendricks
Scat a Thad Jones solo and catching
Brando in The Fugitive Kind
It's playing above your sleep

The weather inside the movie
Is like the weather of life
It rains in black and white

Outside the walls of
Kaiser-Permanente
The silence is dry
The drought drags on

El Paso Monologue

Mexico needs mahogany
and I plan to sell it to them
They're too far north to have
their own
It's not as cold as
it is in Yucatan
New Guinea
50 degrees year around
My men can't go swimmin'
Lots of elk and deer
because we killed off
their natural enemies
Bears and panthers
Bobcats aren't strong
enough to get rid of them
The lakes have sunk
twenty feet and so
because they can't hide
from the birds
the fish supply has
been depleted
I'd like to set up
some businesses in
Russia

They have the most
trees outside of South
America
But nobody knows what's
going to happen there
Those people are like
the woodpeckers who
leave holes in our trees
Absolutely no concept
of private property

Memphis

You can't have it both ways
A sleek red wing tipping
the 21st century
A bloody Confederate boot
in the 19th
You boast all of the
trappings of civilization
The Peabody Hotel with its
duck promenade and
chocolate minted
pillows
The Beale Street of
flocking tourists
Your bar-be-cue beer
and The Blues
Your Civil Rights
Museum where you can
board a Montgomery
bus and sit in the back
and Graceland
Home of the man
who couldn't growl like
Big Mama Thornton

Memphis
Your river is known
far and wide
They tell me that you
can get a direct flight
to Amsterdam from here
They show me the courtroom
where "The Firm" was shot

So Memphis, why don't I
feel good about visiting here
Why with all of these things
going for you, do you
erect a statue to General Nathan
Forrest
Founder of the Klan
Killer of Negroes
at Fort Pillow
Axe Murderer
What is wrong with
your heart, Memphis
that you would
honor such a man?
Will you one day build
a statue to
Richard Speck

adorned with eight
strangled Angels?

Or what about
Jeffery Dahmer
Will you erect one to
him
With the epitaph
"He served mankind"

I am not the walrus

"I am the walrus," The Beatles

I am not the walrus
I am the virus
your insides are my supper
you are defenseless against me
your science impotent
your antibiotics
I trick them
I am not the walrus
I am the virus
Wipe that smile off your face
this is serious
I can make you delirious
spending all of your
waking hours in the can
Nobody can give you a hand
I am not the walrus
I am the virus
I can render you incapable
of eating
of loving
When I get finished with you
you will curse the day you

were born
Your mother, your father
your god cannot help you
I spit on your god
I will make you hot all over
I will send you chills
Your bills will pile up
You will bleed from every
hole in your body
O, you think that I am
ugly
Just for that I will
pock up your pretty face
You will put food into
your throat path
I will block the path
Population control
Get out of the way
I'll show you how
to deal with that
Your body will shrink
like a popped balloon
I will follow you into the
ground
I will fight the bugs
Over you

You are mine
You belong to me
I am not the walrus
I am the virus

Love Crime

When I came home you
were in the dining room
you'd had a couple of
shots and you were crying
I asked you what happened and
you told me

that you didn't
know a nurse was
supposed to be present when
a gynecologist examined you

I went to his house
I was so mad the steering
wheel was shaking
I knocked out his Doberman
I disarmed his alarm system
I waited for him to come home
And he finally did
Driving up in an obnoxious
Utility Wagon
4 miles to the gallon
He was whistling a tune
A tune that I hate

A tune from a bad musical
When he got to the door
of his 3 million dollar
Tudor home
I came up from behind the bushes
He didn't recognize me
in my Mickey Mouse mask

I treated his throat the
way he treated your cervix
I wrote some graffiti on
his garage door
The police will call it
a hate crime
But they will have it wrong

In Bahia

In Bahia's
where I want to be
In Bahia
on a beach by the sea
There's a girl there
she's got hemp for hair
In Bahia
She's waiting for me

In Bahia
they worship the sun
In Bahia
They dance till they're done
There's a girl there
She's got hemp for hair
In Bahia
She's waiting for me

In Bahia
We'll have a parade
In Bahia
We'll make love for days
There's a girl there
She's got hemp for hair

In Bahia
She's waiting for me

In Bahia
Invisibles are seen
In Bahia
Yemaja is queen
There's a girl there
She's got hemp for hair
In Bahia
She's waiting for me

Got my red mask
Got my white suit and tie
Got my drums packed
and I'm ready to fly
There's a girl there
She's got hemp for hair
In Bahia
She's waiting for me

Azabu kissaten de / At an Azabu Cafe
(Japanese / English)

Azabu kissaten de
Anata ni tegami o kakimasu
Azabu kissaten de
Watashi no inki wa namida desu
Azabu kissaten de
Mai ban koko ni suwarimasu
Azabu kissaten de
Watashi no gohan wa tabako desu
Azabu kissaten de
Wastashi no mizu wa uisukii desu

At an Azabu cafe
I write a letter to you
At an Azabu cafe
Tears are my ink
At an Azabu cafe
I sit here night after night
At an Azabu cafe
Cigarettes are my food
At an Azabu cafe
Whiskey is my water
I write a letter to you
At an Azabu cafe

Ole
(Yoruba)

Ole
Ku-u' le o!
wahala m ni yi
abuku mi ni yi
ipo-oku mi ni yi
mo fun o ni gbogbo e

Ole
Ku-u' le o!
idaamu mi ni yi
ese mi ni yi
aibale-okan mi ni yi
ego mi ni yi
aimokan mi ni yi
Mo fun o ni gbogbo e

Ole
Ku-u' le o!
Ohun-ini mini yi
Ola mi ni yi
Ife mi ni yi
Iro mi ni yi
Otito inu mi ni yi
Emi mi ni yi
N o ba o ja feyii!

Thief

(English)

Thief
Greetings!
This is my trouble
This is my disgrace
This is my hell
I give them to you

Thief
Greetings!
This is my confusion
This is my sin
This is my crisis
This is my stupidity
This is my ignorance
I give them to you

Thief
Greetings!
These are my valuables
This is my honor
This is my love
This is my imagination
This is my truth
This is my spirit
I will fight you for these!

Mo Ku Lana / Mo Jinde Loni
(Yoruba)

Mo ku lana
Mo jinde loni

Mo ku lana
Mo ti je 'po
Mo jinde loni
Mo ti j' eja oboku
Mo ku lana
Mo jinde loni
Mo ku lana
Mo ti r' awon gunnugun
Mo jinde loni
Mo ti r' awon adaba
Mo ku lana
Mo jinde loni
Mo ku lana
Mo ti mu petepete
Mo jinde loni
Mo ti mu waini
Mo ku lana
Mo jinde loni
Mo ku lana
Mo jinde loni

Mo ku lana

Mo jinde loni

Mo ku lana

Mo ko le korin

Mo jinde loni

Mo n' korin yii

Mo n' korin yii

Mo n' korin yii

Mo n' korin yii

I Died Yesterday / I Rose Today
(English)

I died yesterday

I rose today

I died yesterday

I ate weed

I rose today

I ate delicious fish

I died yesterday

I rose today

I died yesterday

I saw vultures

I rose today

I saw doves

I died yesterday

I rose today

I died yesterday

I drank mud

I rose today

I drank wine

I died yesterday

I rose today

I died yesterday

I rose today

I died yesterday

I rose today
I died yesterday
I could not sing
I rose today
I'm singing this song
I'm singing this song
I'm singing this song
I'm singing this song

Tough Love

Turning the welfare system
over to the states is like
turning Frank Sinatra over
to Ernest Borgnine in
From Here to Eternity

untitled

He may be your God
but he nothin but a
a white man with stringy dirty hair
to me
wait till Juba come back
we'll see about this
we'll see about all of this
that hymnal they gave you
with these bleak songs
the lies in that book
when Juba comes back
we'll straighten you out
when Juba come back

untitled

Such is the consumer debt
that not only do we rob
Peter to pay Paul
but rob Peter to pay Peter
He owns three credit cards
from American Express
Recently he borrowed from
one that was 9.5% interest
to pay off one that was 18%
Formerly we were sold from
plantation to plantation
Today we're sold from
interest to interest

Tennessee's Revenge

I placed a jug in Connecticut
I figured it could use some good corn
There's more to life than the Stanley Cup
And cricket on the lawn

Now Windsor Locks has ham on
The hocks and Hartford
Dolly Parton

I placed a jug in Delaware
A jar of peach jam wouldn't do
And now there's fiddlin'
In Dover and
And sales are brisk
For Land Rovers

untitled

In Africa, I met a man whose father
hunted elephants
He is an herbalist
In Africa, I met a woman whose
grandmother lived to 120 years
In Africa, there are 55 countries
and 25,000 languages
In Africa black men fly airplanes
run newspapers
When the sun goes home
it goes to Africa

Hotel Agora, Amsterdam

He wasn't
Apricot
But the reflection of the
Rose upon the orange juice

Against the wall
A wounded cello leans

Four Untitled

1

There are black cat fish in the rivers of
Louisiana that will kick a man's brains out

2

Every time you say New Orleans to her
She gains five pounds

3

Ever get the
Feeling that your past
Is a hunter who knows the
Woods better than you

4

Poets have written so
Much about Roses that
Roses have become
Publicity shy

Paper-Weight

It is better to be poor and obscure
Than to be famous and broke
The poor have no need for paper
Newspapers, magazines, paperbacks
Taking over their car trunks
Smelling like a mob victim

Manuscripts have made a nest
Of his couch, chair
And the living room sofa

He hasn't seen his wife in years
She is buried beneath a Sahara
Of papers

He is imprisoned by paper

Had he known that there'd
Be so much paper in his life
He would have been born
A match

untitled

What is it about this man
that the very mention of
his name causes me to
lock the car keys inside
the car

Ichiban Suki

(Japanese)

Anata ga suki desu
Ame ga furu toki

Anata wa Watashi no
Akai kasa desu

Anata ga suki desu

Oba ga suki dewa arimasen
Soshite, Anata ga suki desu

Anata wa
Kanemochi no oji desu

Watashi wa
Tamanegi ga suki dewa arimasen
Anata ga suki desu
Anata wa kireina daikon desu

Ichiban suki

Anata ga suki desu
Kono mokuroku ga suki dewa
Arimasen
Kono mokuroku yori
Anata ga suki desu

Number 1
(English)

I love you
When it rains

You are my red umbrella
I love you

I don't like my aunt
But I love you

You are my rich uncle
I don't like onions
I love you
You are a beautiful white radish

You are number one

I love you
I don't like this list
You are more than this list

The South Berkeley Branch Closes

They closed down the branch
That served black neighborhoods
Now, the elderly from the
Harriet Tubman Homes and the
Sojourner Truth Manor
Have to taxi to
The middle aged
Urban professionals'
Branch
It will take extra pains for
Them to make deposits and withdrawals
Located near latte cafes
And ice cream parlors
Boutiques, art cinemas
Gourmet supermarkets
And salons
You can get your legs waxed
There for forty dollars
There will be even longer
Delays when I cash my check
They will make phone calls to
See whether I am whom I say
I am
The bank manager will look

Up at me as the clerk shows
Her my signature
The bank guard will glare at me
I have been their customer
For over 25 years
I won't go anywhere near
Their new location
I stick out like a sore
Thumb in this neighborhood
Plain-clothes men will follow me
Wherever I go and
Video cameras
VHS my every move
Pale pale women will dog my path
Traveling from my house
To this part of town
Will become a Freedom Ride

Senior Citizens

There were as many sparrows
on their Holly tree
as red berries
Their Holly tree
Couldn't spare a sparrow
Chorus after chorus
they went on and on
Despite their dull gray
coats
they sang like Mockingbirds
on this Holly tree
their Minton's

Twenty years ago,
Luther and Jesse
stood before this tree
She had just gotten her
hair done
It was black and brilliant
A new dress made her body shine
His chest was thrust out
Luther was smiling
He wore a clean starched shirt
They were robust, prime
and proud

Twenty years later
I saw them
Luther was stumbling into
their home, pushing his
portable oxygen tank ahead of
him. The doctor said
that without it
he would "expire"
He had just enough breath
to tell me that he would
quit smoking
Jesse was following
Every step she took hurt
Her body had just about
given out

Because they were fifty
dollars above the poverty line
they were not eligible
for assistance
That week they had to
rush him to the hospital
The ambulance cost $800
Generations of school children
depended upon her
She nurtured them

and read them stories
Taught them how to count
called on them when they raised their hand
He was a longshoreman
lifting heavy at the Port of
Oakland
Unloading ships from Africa
Asia and South America
Luther drove a taxi for thirty years
but was never a hack
They made him wear a uniform
and fight yellow people in the Pacific
but he couldn't do mess
with his white comrades

When he sat on the porch
gazing out on 53rd St
I wonder was he thinking about
his honorable discharge
and how the country he fought for
left him and Jesse flat on their backs

At the end they were dependent upon
the neighbors to do
their shopping
empty the garbage

open a window
take them to the hospital
mail their letters
assist them in the toilet
fetch Luther a Big Mac

They took turns getting sick

Luther finally did die
Her relatives came and
took Jesse to Pasadena
The birds deserted the
Holly tree
Their petunias died

This is what happens to
you nowadays
If you stay around
too long

Guys

Guys
Do you know
what forensics experts
say?
Every time two people
encounter each other
they leave something
behind

Guys
Your women are keeping
things from you
Make them yield
property that only you
should claim
Make them list
the names of all of
their lovers
Track these lovers down
Dispossess them of what
is rightfully yours
No matter how microscopic
No matter how vague
a sigh

a confidence
No matter how circumstantial
the whispers they've
shared with your women
what went on in the dark
Make them cough up old
kisses
and passionate sweats

Guys
Beat the devil out of these men
until they come clean
Conduct a thorough search
of their memories
You should begin
immediately
before the trail gets cold

untitled

I'd rather have my short term memory back
than win a vintage Eldorado Cadillac

Let Oakland Be a City of Civility

Let Oakland be a city of civility
Let each citizen treat other
citizens with good will and
generosity

Let Oakland be a city of civility
in dealings no matter how small
let the cars stop as soon as a
pedestrian steps from the curb
Let Oakland be a city of civility

Let unleashed pit bulls be removed
from the streets
let the dog owners clean up
after their dogs
and the litterers clean up
after their litter
let Oaklanders treat the streets
as though they were their living rooms
let people refrain from copping an
attitude when asked to turn their
boom boxes down
let road rage and excessive honking be
removed from our public life
Let Oakland be a city of civility

Let those who are packing AK47s
and Uzis move to another town
let the Superflies who use our
teenagers as prostitutes and
crack dealers move with them
let their suburbanite customers
stay home in the suburbs with their
wives and children
let the gun dealers stay there too

Let suburbanites treat Oakland with
respect instead of a place
they invade in the morning
and leave with the money at night
Let Oakland be a city of civility

Let the pupils respect the teachers
and let the teachers respect the students
no matter which English they choose to
express themselves
let the students respect each other
let their test scores shoot through the roof
let them go on to college in record numbers
let achieving As and Bs be as important as scoring
jump shots

Let Oakland be a city of civility
Let our sports teams be jubilant, but humble
in victory and graceful in defeat
Let Oakland be a city of civility

Let the police be courteous to all of the
citizens and the citizens be
courteous to the police
let the women of Oakland go through
life without receiving a single slap punch or kick
Let us discipline our children with moderation
let the hungry be fed and the homeless
removed to rooms, apartments and houses
let neighborhood development
be as important as downtown development

Let cooperation, beauty and peace
characterize our neighborhoods
and let their trees, flowers and gardens
be cultivated
let our hotels be filled to capacity
let our convention centers be teeming
with delegates
let jobs be as abundant
as geese in Oakland's estuary
let our senior citizens be

treated with dignity and reverence
for they are our walking libraries
let them play bocce ball
do Tai Chi
mentor our children
and get lucky in Reno
Let Oakland be a city of civility

Let our cultural bouillabaisse cook
Let our Symphony regale us
Let the Blues blow us away
Let our Jazz clubs be smoking
Let our painters mural our history
Let our dancers fascinate us with
arabesques, tap, stomps, Jazz dance
Modern dance, Neo-African dance, Mambo
Salsa and Cha Cha Cha
Let our Hip-Hoppers break-dance
rap and graffiti
Let us resuscitate ourselves
with teriyaki, couscous
curry lamb, fettuccini, pizza, red
beans and rice, hot links and gumbo
Let Oaktown be Gumbo city
but let our waistlines narrow
Let us bubble over with verve

Let us be visionary with ALL-Get-Out
Let us be beside ourselves
with Civic Pride

And though we are all Oaklanders
let us remember where we come from
China, Korea, Japan, Taiwan, the
Philippines, India, Mexico, the Middle East,
Africa, Europe, Hawaii, Oklahoma,
Arkansas, Texas and Louisiana
Let us ratchet up our goals
Let the blood in our veins be pumping
Let our hearts beat strong
Let Oakland be a city of civility
Let the good times roll

Our Love Was Like a Forest Fire

Our love was like a forest fire
drawing help from 13 states
Our love was like a forest fire
drawing help from 13 states
But our heat was so far out
of control
that the help arrived too late

We stalked each other from bar to bar
You spent the grocery money and you
Stole my car
The finance company is trying to
track me down
You burned the furniture
and you brought me down
The laughing stock all over
town

Our love was like a forest fire
drawing help from 13 states
Our love was like a forest fire
drawing help from 13 states
But our heat was so far out

of control
that the help arrived too late

Look like a red sash around
my body
look like a rash is on my
neck
Got a gash
that required ten stitches
had to sell my Cadillac
Got A HICKEY THAT'S PLAIN TO SEE
but instead of saying I'm sorry
you called the law on me

There's nobody at your party
Your fame has come and gone
Nobody's buying what you're selling
You're going broke each day
They don't want you in Philly
They don't want you in L.A.
You too old to do the Hip Hop
and you ain't no Lady Day

You're back now where
you started

in our two room railroad shack
But before we started to fighting
we tumbled into the sack

I guess you people are tired
of hearing
that same old plaintive song
of one lover telling everybody
how the other one did wrong
But there's two sides to every
story or maybe three or four
The way we hurt each other
Yet reached each other's core

So I'm saying goodbye forever
I'm packing my bags and gone
I'll take that Amtrak
at midnight
The Buffalo to New York
run
you won't see me forever
and don't be sending me
no gram
this is what you get
for the malice in your bones

I'm all out of making up
I'm exhausted and I'm done
I'm tired of being your bum
My friends think I'm dumb
Go find you another woman
That you can twirl around your
thumb
somebody wide eyed and trusting
somebody who will take your flak
I'm going far far way from here
and i ain't comin back

untitled

the reason for his unsmiling
            self-portraits?
Van Gogh killed himself
    because he felt that sooner
    or later his paintings would
    be displayed in a Las Vegas hotel

Double Diagnosis

When your mother was
pregnant
She said "I'm eating
for two"

Now that you're
42
I'm thinking for two

untitled

This poem came at me
like a flash flood
If I had paused to count meter
I would have drowned

untitled

Do you think that a hippo gives
a poke about whether its ancestor
is a whale or a pig
Do you think that a pig in its brig
worries about its ultimate sausage fate
Does it matter to a chicken whether you
think it's ugly
Does a squirrel after devouring
a mouse whole regret that it
forgot to don a napkin
Have you ever seen a fish shopping
for deodorant
or an ant loitering

we are superior to the lower animals aren't we

untitled

If being associated with Buffalo doesn't
bother Niagara Falls
why should it be a big problem
for you

In A War Such Things Happen

We were eating black bread and
drinking goat's milk when your
missile hit our house
I am the only survivor
and when I asked you why
you said well this is war
and in a war such things
happen

They gave us ten minutes to
leave because your army
was within the city limits
the young one got lost and
when we found her she
said that eight of your men
took turns with her and now
all day she stares into space
and takes pills whose names
I can't pronounce and when
I asked you why you said
well this is war
and in a war such things
happen

You said that if we surrendered
you would give us cigarettes and
chocolate but instead
you put us in a place fit for
hens and when I asked why
you said
well this is war
and in a war such things happen

You bombed a bus because you
said your enemy was inside but
when we told you that they were
simple farmers instead you apologized
and said, well this is war and in war
such mistakes happen

You told a press conference
that these men had engaged
you in a firefight. You
lied didn't you. When
we did the autopsies we
found that their throats had
been cut and there were no
weapons in their possession
and when we asked you why

you said, well this is war
and in a war such things happen

You hit those twin towers
because you wanted to address
the powerful, but you killed
secretaries, waitresses, janitors
busboys, dishwashers and civil
servants and when we asked you
why, you said, well this is war
and you wanted to make a point

She had just graduated from college
and was about to be wed
You sent her into a
restaurant. She blew herself up,
killing families who were enjoying
a Sunday afternoon and when
we asked you why you said well
this is war and such things happen

You said that your weapons
were so precise that you could
land a missile in a coffee cup
yet scores of people lie wounded

dying and dead in the market
and when we asked you what
happened, you said that this
is the nature of war and in a
war mistakes occur

After 20 hours of digging we
removed the rubble
We found the bits of rotting
flesh
We knew it was a child
from the size of its rib cage
We knew that it was my son
from the red Nike sneaker
You said you were after suicide
bombers
He was 3 years old
You said that this was war
and in a war, such things happen

A million years passed
Herds of rhinoceroses, elephants
and lions roamed the African
plains
There were more cheetahs than
you could shake a stick at

You could see to the bottom of
the rivers with the naked
eye
Snow had returned to Kilimanjaro
The oceans were filled with
whales, tuna, swordfish, sharks
The glaciers were once again
solid and imposing
The Amazon rain forest was
chirping away
Trees covered the city where
glass buildings once stood
A bear met a wolf
in the thick forest and
the bear asked
"What became of those creatures who
used to shoot us for sport
furnish their wives with the
fur off our backs
terrorize our young
put their saws to our
homes?"
"They had a war," the wolf said
galloping off, "and in a war such things happen."

Lenny

You loved it so
you could taste it
It was your bread and
butter
Your cream potatoes
and Halibut
It could make you
leap for joy
sob in public
say inappropriate things
engage in inappropriate
actions
which once brought you
a reprimand from a
reporter
he was from the
Wall Street Journal
You remind me of your
complex antecedent
like you
He wore his music on
his sleeves
He was controversial
odd

Can you imagine
Symphony wives gossiping
while Gustav Mahler
peered from behind the
curtains

America United

They are saying that we should join hands and show
solidarity with our new friends,
That we should burn candles and sing "God Bless
America" and "Amazing Grace" and stand tall
with Sir Rudolph Giuliani, the Mayor of New York
The Joker among Racial Profilers, under whose
rule 35 thousand Hispanic and Black Men
were stopped and frisked
"No one group should be targeted
as a result of the WTC bombing," Sir Giuliani said
They say that we should link arms with the
killers of Amadou Diallo, shot 44 times while
minding his own business
That we should march with
them to that gleaming City on the Hill, preceded
by the Albany jury that acquitted them, who
play "Yankee Doodle Dandy" on their piccolos
fifes and drums
They say that we should form a big strong line
with Sir Colin Powell who said that he's
against the bombing of civilians and buildings
"I'm against the bombing of civilians and buildings,"
said Secretary of State Powell, MacWorld's Black Knight
They say that we should show our gratitude to the

woman whom President George Bush, Jr. calls Condi as in
"Get me Condi"
Ms. Condoleezza Rice, daughter of the
Hoover Institute and Chevron Oil,
murderer of the Nigerian Delta people
He calls upon her when he lacks the facts
which is often
Maybe we should send her a carton of
nail polish hot combs skin lighteners
and pocket mirrors to show
our gratitude, our affection
She said that there was no reason for
The US to attend the Race conference in Durban
South Africa
She said that "We are a country that does not
judge people by their skin color or religious
beliefs"
They say that we should bow our heads and pray along
with George Dumya Bush, who said that the
citizens of South Carolina should decide whether
the Confederate flag should fly over the state capitol
who said that every black man who was electrocuted
in Texas received a fair trial
He said that he wanted the "evil doers"
"Dead or Alive," smirking, eyes squinting
Send them all to Boot Hill

which is how we do it in Texas
why shucks, we're going to smoke
them out of their holes because
they're the bad guys and we're
the good guys so
you're either with us or you're
with them
He said that he would bomb Afghanistan
as soon as Condi showed him where it was
on the map
Bombs upon which they write "Hijack this, fag"
Because they is the man
they is civilized
And they cluster bomb hundreds of men, women and
    children
because they are with them
And they bomb the Red Cross because
they are with them
And they bomb hospitals and senior citizens' homes
because they are with them
And they bomb thousands of goats, sheep, pheasants,
donkeys and geese because they are with them
Osama Bin Laden who, if he is a modem equipped
cave ogre, had his fangs, hooves and horns supplied
by American taxpayers
If the Russians had built a bigger soccer
stadium we would have even more room

to punish women who read books and don't
cover their ankles!

Dumya Bush, Bin Laden's comrade-in-oil, thinks
All I wanted to be was baseball commissioner
but hell being president is more of a blast than I thought.
Every time I open my mouth, thousands flee their
homes and head for the borders. When I visited Italy
a few months ago, the police beat up demonstrators
while shouting "Il Duce." Who is this Il Duce? Get me
Condi.
They say that we should place flags in our
windows and join Dumya in his
Crusade, I mean campaign
They say that we should bond with
the neo-Confederates and All-American Union Busters
Trent Lott, John Ashcroft, Gale Norton and
maybe join them in burning a cross because
that's what brotherhood means, doesn't it
joining together
and standing around fires and stuff
Won't Generals Nathan B. Forrest, Robert E. Lee
and Stonewall Jackson, American patriots all
be proud of us and
beam up to us from their permanent residence
as we stand shoulder to shoulder with Dixie

I got it. Maybe we would fly the Stars and Bars
along with the Stars and Stripes to
show that not only is one country united
but both countries, I mean shucks
two for one is a good deal ain't it
Ain't that what they say at Wal-Mart
They say that we should chant
USA! USA! with people
who shadow us down the aisles
of department stores, hassle us
for living while black
who voted for Proposition 209, 187
and 21, who try our children as adults
and place them in jail with predators
They say that we should chant *USA! USA!*
with people who say that it's the poor's
fault that they are poor
They say that we should chant *USA! USA!*
with people who drag us from behind pickup trucks
and beat us for taking a walk in Bensonhurst, New York
People who
send our kids to special education classes
who say racism doesn't exist
It's just us playing the race card
Why don't we sing "America, The Beautiful"
with those who red line
and gentrify us into oblivion

Why don't we join Gov. Gray "Lights Out" Davis
who reduced our community colleges' budget
by millions
and Jerry Brown, the Imperial Mayor of
Oakland, in a recitation of
the Pledge of Allegiance
I mean, police brutality is the price you
have to pay to get people to shop at the
Gap
They say that we should stand with
Rev. Billy Graham
Pat Robertson and Jerry Falwell
Christian soldiers
who want to hammer the infidels
"Why those people over there are
Manicheans. They see the world in
black and white," said Stephen Cohen from the
Brookings Institute
They say that we should belt out a chorus of
"Cumbaya" with
Pfizer Pharmaceuticals, experimenters on
African children, applaud them
for donating to the recovery effort of those thousands
who perished at the WTC
sacrificed on the chainsaw of ignorance and
arrogance, the twin brothers of mayhem and death

They say that we should give a warm patriotic
embrace to those who say they're fighting for
freedom abroad but deny us freedom at home
they always say that
"we're fighting for freedom"
They said it during World War I, World War II
The Korean War, the Vietnam War and the Gulf
War
They say now Mose and Mosetta and
Li'l Abner and Daisy Mae
Jose and Maria if you
die for us in the steaming stinking jungles
and in the mean Afghanistan winters
we'll maybe let you
have a grilled cheese sandwich at Denny's

They say that we should unite
That we should display the flag
wear red white and blue headrags
and help rebuild Wall Street
"More than two weeks after the
terrorist attacks, costume retailers
report that the good guys are out-
selling the bad. Grownups and kids
are bypassing black capes and picking
up patriotic gear such as Uncle Sam

hats."
They say we should empty our pockets and max out
our credit cards on Christmas
to show our loyalty
"We must not put our buying
decisions on hold. Go out and
buy cars, and automobiles, and
electronics, and appliances," said
the economist.
"The market is a forward looking
beast. We must hunker down with
the Beast," she said
"Santa is going to look a lot
like Uncle Sam this year," predicted
Monk Rivers, a spokesman for the
Mill Corporation, which operates 12
malls
We should show our determination
to vanquish our enemy
by emptying our wallets
We must hunker down with the beast
for this Crusade, I mean campaign
Operation Noble Eagle I mean
Operation Infinite Justice
I mean Operation Enduring Freedom
I mean—

as soon as we can find out
who the enemy is
Their unpronounceable names
Their strange customs
Their scraggly beards
Their writing that looks like
wriggling worms
Their baggy pants
The diapers on their heads
By jiminy, I heard that these A-rabs
expect to be surrounded by
25 virgins when they blow
themselves to kingdom come
They hate modernity
They hate *Pink Flamingos*
Britney Spears
theme parks, diet Coke, corn syrup sucrose
obesity and novels whose
length exceed 500 pages
Why can't they get with the program

"WHY DO THEY HATE US?"
Major David Letterman asked General Dan Rather
"THEY HATE US BECAUSE THEY'RE EVIL
THEY HATE US BECAUSE THEY'RE ENVIOUS"
said General Dan Rather from his blow dried and

tanned silver foxhole at Black Rock
"Let The President Tell Me Where To Go
and I'll show up," he said
"We should invade their countries
kill their leaders and convert
them to Christianity," said Admiral Ann Coulter
the *Daily News*'s ersatz blonde
We should join Dumya in his crusade
I mean his campaign as soon as we can
locate the enemy. It keeps changing
like a chameleon. It seems to be always
one camp, or cave ahead of us
What did the woman on C-Span say
on Sept. 23, phoning in to *Washington Journal*
"Where do I go to get the understanding of
what I need to understand
in order to understand the president?"

Who wants to invade Afghanistan or is
it Pakistan
or is it Tajikistan or is it
Uzbekistan or is it
Turkmenistan?
I can't stand all of these stands
Hey, don't we have someone who can speak Arabic?
Hey! What happened to those shining

seas that were supposed to protect us
from all of this PC nonsense?
All I wanted was to be baseball commissioner
Get me Condi!

I Want to Be a Right Wing Family Values Type of Man

I want to be a right wing
family values type of man
frequent all the porno and
smut shops that I can
Lecture the ghettos about
their promiscuity
While giving some hot babe
some hootchie coochie
I want to be a right wing
family values type of man

I want to be a right wing
family values type of man
preach that the drug laws
shouldn't bend
But you'd find me in Georgetown
snorting coke
any weekend
I want to be a right wing
family values type of man

I want to be a right wing
family values type of man
Insist that low street crimes
be brought to the docket
while easing a little soft money
into my expensive suit pocket
I want to be a right wing
family values type of man

I want to be a right wing
family values type of man
You'd see me in campaign ads
with my wife, dog and child
But when partying with the
boys, I'd get a little wild
Have strippers and drag
queens coming out the ears
after doing more than a half-
dozen beers,
But tomorrow I'm in Congress
raising morals and
Because I'd be a right wing
family values type of man

Imenhoptep

The world may run out of water
and the world may run out of oil
but the world will never run out of
tourists.

They arrive in Egypt with bottled water
Aqua, Schweppes and Baraka
digitalized hordes
They cling to their camera bags
and grip their sunglasses
In Luxor, they pay good money
to crawl into the spaces of the dead
whose tombs have been removed
they chatter in a dozen languages
gazing at figures that are half
human and half animal or bird
they wander about statues
that have survived every invasion
every defacement
from the graffiti of the Greeks
vandalism by Christians to
the mad Turk who shot off
the Sphinx's nose
Aggressive souvenir peddlers

pester the invaders with
mementoes
and invitations to shop for
perfume and papyrus and to
see where the alabaster is made
They'll sell you a statue of Ba
for $300 instead of the fortune
it's worth because they can't
authenticate its being found in
a tomb
The waiters at the Movenpick hotel
cater to the visitors from Japan
and England
who watch the sun set
over the Nile to the accompaniment
of Tchaikovsky's *Swan Lake*
The children sell clay statues of
the Sphinx
the salespeople at the Thomas Cook
travel agency can book you into Giza
the guides lure their clients
into restaurants and businesses for
a percentage of the take
The people at the Osiris Bazaar
the people at the Isis Tours and Hotels
the guards at the Egyptian Museum

earn their keep by
scolding you for using a flash camera
Everybody got paid

Imenhoptep designed the first
pyramid and for his effort
received only
room and board

What further proof do we need
That the ancient Egyptians were black

He Picked a Fight With Haitians

I cost my master nothing
I don't eat, I don't get tired
I don't sleep
At night, I lurch through
cemeteries
During the day, I work
carrying water for my victims
picking beans
feeding the chickens
gathering sticks for fire
walking barefoot through
the valley
And my hands don't crack
or bleed
fungi, sores and slime
cover my body
I cannot smell my rot
Flies have built colonies
on my stinking clothes
I have no use for a heart
My soul cannot catch
up with me
I cannot enjoy
this beautiful land

located east of Santo
Domingo
Cannot enjoy the birds
with rainbows pasted to
their feathers
Cannot enjoy the
aggressive insistent
Bougainvillea
Cannot enjoy the
Caldoza
the Ahioka
the Checkere
All I have left from my
former career is the badge
they buried me with
You see
I was once the chief
of police

When I Die I Will Go to Jazz

"Jazz Is My Religion" (Ted Joans)

As Ted would say
Let them go to heaven
or let them go to Hell
when I die I want to go to Jazz

Who needs Gabriel when we got
Clifford, Clark, Lee and Bix
You can add Thad
to that distinguished mix
and Prez and Billy sit on
their thrones
and their court wear porkpies
gardenias and checkered vests
And the tempo of the place is
like Denzil Best
With Mingus and Ray Brown doing
the chores on bass

A place where Satch is Avatar
and Sun Ra, Gil and Count
are resident Sages

and among those on trumpet
are Fats and Hot Lips Page

With Klook on drums and
and Trane on Axe
a thousand years of
Jamming
for what more could I
ask

Let them go to heaven
let them go to Hell
when I die I want to go to Jazz
Don't surround me with cherubim
with their golden locks
a place where there's no vodka
on the rocks
and spare me the diet of
milk and honey
in this high-up Lincoln Center
where it's all about the money

What use are Angels
singing a cappella
When I can have Dinah, Sarah and

a scatting Ella
A tisket a tasket I lost
my yellow basket
Mr. Paganini please play
my melody
I want to spend eternity in
a place where they can swing it
No need for a Paradise where
anybody can wing it
The folks in Jazz
might not dress in
white garments but
they're as natty and clean as
a stylish Earl Garner
Or Duke in his tails, gloves
and black top hat
and Saint Peter is Babs Gonzales
saying welcome home
cats

The residents of Jazz are
bopping in the aisles
As Diz and Bird swap
fours with Miles
And spare me the sounds
of celestial harmonics

I prefer something like
Jazz at the Philharmonic
Jumping with my boy Sid
in the city

When I die I will go
straight to Jazz
No need for me to encounter
The Naz and
Don't send me off with
No Razz a Ma Tazz
some bars from Round
Midnight will do just fine
and lacking that
some Earl Father Hines

Bad Mouth

The entrance to hell is not a
dark cave
The entrance to hell is your mouth
Bats fly from between your teeth
and your tongue is the breeding ground
for lice

Your tongue is more than forked
It is a wild red snake that won't be
tamed
It's a switchblade made of membrane
slashing one's character and one's fame
It is a serial killer
with foul breath
the stench of its victims
Your mouth is a dirty hole
into which rats escape
They do their business there

I've seen your mouth drive the unwed
mother to throw a fetus into the trash
The gay teenager to gas himself
Innocent men on death row are
there because of your mouth

It is the original jailhouse informer
It is the stoolie, the fink

Your mouth is a desert
barren but for the bones of dead men

A dead man stood before my
bed last night
it was about a quarter past 3
I can't stay for long he said
Just look what the mouth did to me
Just look
I had a nice home, two kids and
plenty of cash
a vacation home in wine country
and some gold that I'd stashed
My life was of bliss
and my soul was at rest
Among those in my field
I ranked with the best
The mouth spread a lie
that chewed up my life
I lost everything, home, kids
and wife
When you see the mouth
coming, don't run away

that's what I did and it
made me its sap

I took his advice and prepared
for the day
when I would take charge
and shut up its trap
When the mouth came to get me
Drooling with lies
boasting and vowing to
dig me a grave
it got there before me
it has nothing to say
it dug its own grave
murdered by its own bad taste

Going East

Elsewhere,
a babe's first words might be
mama or dada
In Berkeley,
babies are born in a
lotus position
Their first word is karma
There might be more
Buddhists in Berkeley than
in Tibet
Some are from Tibet
but many are from
Brooklyn
Bishop George Berkeley
you got it backwards
It's "Go East, Young Man,
Go East."

Hands On

In the 1930s
they were slopping hogs
in Anniston, Alabama and
starching Arrow shirts on
Lookout Mountain
In the 1940s, they
built GM cars from the
axle up and joined unions
He is the first Professor
in a family whose admiration
goes to people who
work with their hands
(His youngest brother is
a carpenter)
and so when
the press asked his mother
for a comment
on the day
that he discovered
the origin
of the universe
she said
"Ah. But can he make a cabinet."

Tokyo Woman Blues

I got an American woman
who likes to fight
from the time we rise in the
morning till we go to bed
at night
I want to get out
but where would I go
maybe hop a plane to
Tokyo
hikoki o norimasu
Tokyo ni ikimasu
hikoki o norimasu
Tokyo ni ikimasu

Tokyo women are
mighty fine
make a man feel like
he's half divine
I got one who is mine
all mine
hikoki o norimasu
Tokyo ni ikimasu
hikoki o norimasu
Tokyo ni ikimasu

I gave her a Lexus
some stocks and a
diamond ring
a Caribbean cruise
a Parisian fling
what did she do
complain and complain
hikoki o norimasu
Tokyo ni ikimasu
hikoki o norimasu
Tokyo ni ikimasu

You can find American
women at the shopping mall
trying on things from stall to
stall
and when they're not
there, they're underneath
the dryer or doing lunch with
their chatty friends
and gossiping about
people's sins
hikoki o norimasu
Tokyo ni ikimasu
hikoki o norimasu
Tokyo ni ikimasu

Some of these American women
spoiled as they can be
stay out all night at the disco
too tired to deal with me
spend billions of dollars
on botox
while their homeless sisters
bleed
they're got the world in a half nelson
yet need and need and need
hikoki o norimasu
Tokyo ni ikimasu
hikoki o norimasu
Tokyo ni ikimasu

The way they raise their
children is a low down
dirty shame
a bunch of thugs and
hookers who will call
you out your name
they sack their parents' purses
to purchase amphetamine
and their ugly noisy music
will make your head insane
hikoki o norimasu

Tokyo ni ikimasu
hikoki o norimasu
Tokyo ni ikimasu

Tokyo women are
mighty fine
make a man feel like
he's half divine
I got one who is mine
all mine
hikoki o norimasu
Tokyo ni ikimasu
hikoki o norimasu
Tokyo ni ikimasu

Prayer for Earth

Speak louder Apocalypse
We can't hear you in the back
Shouted out the audience of
Stetson hats
(from an early discarded poem by I.R.)

If global trends continue
We will be separated from
Our huge waistlines
Our plasma TVs and cell phones
Our oversized vehicles growing
Ever larger so that one day
Each American will own a bus

Earth,
You are
Our first class berth
In space
You are the stomping ground of the human
Race
Designer of Dorothy Dandridge's face
Of the black beaches of Hilo
Of the marble that made Venus de Milo

Thank you for the caps

Of Mount Tacoma

For scallops and the Alps

For George Clinton's funk

For Thelonious Monk

For trumpets and trombones

For Polonaises, Blues and Sonatas

For the Alhambra of Granada

For the bronze of Benin

For Michelangelo's Sistine

For the marketplace at Barcelona

For the evidence of things unseen

For Zimbabwe, Accra, Abuja

And Mandalay Bay

We thank you for

Carmen McRae and

For dolphins at play

For El Greco of Toledo

For the cathedral at Köln

For Damballah, Krishna, and Vishnu

Earth, you have blessed us

And now we must wish you well

And send you

On your journey

With or without us

May you be shamrock green again
May you stay out of the way of black holes
May that asteroid three miles across
That is supposed to hit within ten
Million years
Avoid you at the last
Minute
Like in the movies

May you survive the nuclear deals
May you survive the chemical spills
May you survive the biotechnology
May you survive the peckerwood theology
May the big crunch theory be all wet
May you spin forever without end
May you survive man
May you survive man
Who was full of such promise

Sly and the Family
Stone said that everybody is a star
Who is composed of the
Same minerals as a planet
Nitrogen and iron
But more often than not

We behave like so much hot air

Earth will you cut us loose

Or will you continue

To give us something

To stand on

Inspiration Point, Berkeley

"If you despise this state so
why did you move here?"
I come here to remind myself
The meadows are designed
by Thomas Hart Benton
Underneath the bridge
white sharks are preying
It is a golden door to Singapore
The freighters are bringing
rare mushrooms
The mountain lions are yawning
There are walkers, cyclists and
runners on the trails
I never knew there were so
many shades of trees
The cows and I are black
I don't even mind the radio
towers
From here
you can see everything
but the faults

December in April

In California, every month is April
One night the ex easterners
smuggled in December
(Like the one they have
In New Hampshire)
A giggling
snowball fight broke out
Palm trees became Frost's
white Birches
There was an eruption of
Poinsettias
Lite Rock was replaced with
"Chestnuts roasting by an
open fire"
We treated ourselves to
hot Irish gruel
instead of Granola
We traded in our surfboards
for a toboggan
and passed the cup of
Egg Nog
One man said that he
never knew that the touch

of galoshes could feel like
the taste of Chardonnay
But by dawn, the last
Snowman had melted

We went to the beach

Billionaire of Life

Thelma V. Reed
my mother
You outlived the 20th
Century
where you listened to
Lindbergh land in Paris

You outlived the Concorde
and flew to Hawaii on
Delta
You saw the "Colored Only"
signs come down
and lived to
dine on Boston Chowder
at Red Lobster's

You kicked off your shoes
in the East Room of the
White House and was your
Family's caretaker and
boot camp commander
(You outlived Patton)
Your friends are in glory
Your enemies

that other place
You outlived your
benefactor
Wilson Greatbatch
Buffalo's white angel
in a bowtie
and suit
patterned like
the landscape of Mars
Inventor of the
pace maker
"One of
two major engineering
feats of the last 50
years."

Like John D. Rockefeller
You've outlived your doctors
John D. was the billionaire of dollars
You are the billionaire of life
For what late sultan would not
have given
up his palaces
or tycoon his stocks
mogul, his oil wells
or gambler, his winnings

to get where you are
Thelma V. Reed
at 88
Through you
spirits bring
custom made
Bible verses for those
needing consul
As you sit on your
throne on
Eggert Road
Across the street from
The Family $

Heidegger's Paradox

In the country of the Blonde
the brunette ones are queen
My wife is Brünnhilde ohne pigtails
Like the joke that made Hennie
Youngman famous
"Take my wife—please"

Her eyes are
lynx blue
You have to have the stamina
of a Jesse Owens to bring her
to a climax
Not so with Hannah
While Elfride is teaching aerobics
to her like-haired Überfrauen
I summon Hannah to the attic
First we listen to Fats Waller
Smoke some Chesterfields
Talk some Jaspers
Then I unbutton her

After all. I am the teacher
She is the student
Later she will write about

Augustine's cravings
let me tell you about mine
they come at night
when I'm lying next to my
Wagnerian Sow
I think of you Hannah
the day you entered my office
there was drizzle on the streets
of Freiburg
that Parisian raincoat
the fashionable hat pulled
over your eyes
dark as sturgeon's eggs
dark as Theda Bara's
Too bad the rest of them are
not like you
They speak German with a
Russian accent
Every time I see one of your brethren
sharing a nightclub table with one
of our women
I want to reach for my pistol

Notes on Virginia

I awoke from my slumber
to find her standing over me
the wench held a dagger
She was about to stab me
But I seized her wrist
There was bedlam in
her green eyes

Her Nigerian nose was flaring
        After we struggled
the weapon
from her hand
She spat in my face
Last week I found ground-up glass
in my breakfast
And then the mysterious fire
in my study where I was
editing The Bill of Rights
Her defiance excites me
but I warned her that
if her vain attempts continued
I would put her son on a spit
He was among those wretches
who served dinner tonight and

the impudent Frenchman said
"Why, he looks like you"
He shan't be invited to Monticello
Again

Reedoku
(Japanese / English)

Watashi no kokoro wa
Koware yasui desu
Otoshite kudasai

My heart is breakable
Please drop it

For Peet's Sake

In Alameda County, the whitest tract isn't in the outlying
*   suburbs. It's in progressive, university-town Berkeley*
*   —San Francisco Chronicle*

Pretty soon,
A black man will have to
Present a visa
In order to enter
Berkeley

Even the well-dressed
Ones

But look at it this way
At the downtown Peet's
You get your own
Salesperson

GETHSEMANE PARK

Gethsemane Park

a Gospera

Synopsis

Beelzebub is still furious over the miracle at Gerasenes where Jesus drove the demons from a madman's head and turned them into swine, after which they drowned in the sea. Jesus is, in a sense, bad news for the demon business, by preventing them from getting into people's heads. Beelzebub stalks Mary Magdalene and the denizens of Gethsemane Park, located in an inner city like Oakland's, sowing mischief and waiting to capture Jesus, who never appears in the park, but his spirit is manifest. *Gethsemane Park* addresses the issues of poverty, homelessness, faith, and miracles and how they apply to the selfish and bottom-line United States of the cruel 1990s.

Gethsemane Park was originally written as a libretto as commissioned and developed by the San Francisco Opera Company, after which time the libretto rights were returned to me. In 1997, the late Mona Vaughn Scott, director of the Black Repertory Group Theatre in Berkeley, commissioned a production, and music was composed and directed by Carmen Moore. Another production of the Reed and Moore collaboration was mounted at the Lorraine Hansberry Theater in San Francisco, directed by Stanley Williams, before it moved to New York City and further

critical success at the Nuyorican Poets Cafe (in a produc-
tion directed by Rome Neal, 2000).

Cast
Gethsemane Park Chorus
Beelzebub, Satan's Chief Deputy, Grating Tenor
1st Associate
2nd Associate
3rd Associate
Mary Magdalene, Mezzo or Contralto
Anne, Mary's Mother, mainly speaking (keening musicals
voice)
Martha, Mary's Sister, Lyric Soprano
Lazarus, Mary's Brother, Baritone/Basso
John, Disciple (Mexican), Lead Tenor
James, Disciple (Chinese), High Tenor
Judas, Disciple, Speaking only-preaches, until baritone
near end
Peter, Disciple, Blues singer (Basso/baritone)
Testifying Woman, Miracle Witness
Highway Patrolman, Miracle Witness
3 AFDC Children
Mary the Mother (cum Near Eastern), operatic lyric

Act 1

Scene 1

(Gethsemane Park. Full of what journalists call "underclass people." These are the CHORUS. When they are not singing, they go about their business engaged in conversation, etc. Some lie under cardboard and newspapers. These people are poorly dressed and some are even wearing blankets. There are shopping carts with people's belongings strewn about. A table has been set up from where MARTHA, her mother ANNE, and MARY MAGDALENE are ladling out soup from a huge pot located on the table. As volunteers, they are dressed better than the others. JOHN, JAMES, PETER, LAZARUS, and JUDAS are also present. MARTHA is confined to a wheelchair.)

ALL

(On stage)

Our God is a walking God
He is not one still in stone
Our God is a walking God
He moves through the towns and cities
Through mountains and valleys
He roams
Our God is a walking God
From Galilee to Decapolis
From Jerusalem, Judea, and beyond
From Capernaum to the streets of Rome
Our God is a walking God
No idol with dumb tongues

He moves through the towns and the cities
Through the villages far flung
From Mobile, Alabama
To Youngstown and New York
To Shreveport, Louisiana
To Chattanooga, L.A., and Grand Forks
Our God is a walking God
He is not one still in stone
He moves through the towns and the cities
Our God is a walking god
Our God *(Repeat 6 times)*
A God who can't sit down
Our God *(Repeat 6 times)*
A God who can't sit down
Our God is a walk around God.
From the streets of New York City
      Walking, walking
To the downtown scenes of Motown
      Walking, walking
From the alleyways of Boston, Massachusetts
        To Market Street at Frisco Bay
To Rio, El Salvador, and the streets of old Bombay
To Madrid, Saigon, or Gethsemane Park

MARY
(MARY comes from behind the soup table to Center Stage)
Never thought I'd meet
Such a man
Whose love was so wide and so deep

CHORUS

Who embraces the poor, the young and old,
The whore, the robber, and the Greek
The rebel Jew, the centurion
Are equal in his eyes

MARY

Never thought I'd meet
Such a man
He rid the devils from my head
He made my brother Lazarus rise
He set my soul on fire

CHORUS

As only Jesus could

MARY

And as for these voices
In my head
Are they gone for good
Or are they just
Waiting somewhere
Stalking me
Circling me
Ready to return?

*(Three of BEELZEBUB'S ASSOCIATES rush on and begin to
do a dance encircling MARY. They are dressed in black
leather and Nike shoes. They taunt her. She moves to break*

from the circle but is not unsuccessful. She holds the sides of
her head.)

BEELZEBUB'S ASSOCIATES
(All together)

Where is your precious Jesus now?

He's going to be crucified.

Unsanctified.

Killed like a common thief.

Dishonored. Vilified.

Crowned with thorns.

Made to drink vinegar.

Is he your pimp?

Mary, have you forgotten your heroin?

Still hearing voices?

(fugal) Still hearing voices. Still hearing voices?

Ha ha ha ha

Ha ha ha

Ha ha ha ha

Ha ha ha

(THIRD ASSOCIATE offers MARY her pill bottles. She
knocks them out of his hand. ASSOCIATES laugh a creepy
gremlinlike laugh. They rush off stage. MARY stands alone.)

MARY

I'll not listen to them

My faith will keep me strong

They can't separate me from

My Jesus
Not them or any throng
> *(Start slow rock)*

He brought me from a life of sin
Of waking up with different men
I massage his body with ointment
And soothe him whenever I can
There is no man so beautiful
So holy, blessed, and kind
While sometimes I still hear the demons' voices

MARTHA, MARY, and CHORUS

It's Jesus. Jesus.
It's Jesus that's on my mind.
Jesus, Jesus Precious Jesus
I got Jesus
All on my mind

It's Jesus. Jesus.
It's Jesus that's on my mind.
Fear and trouble don't bother me
I got Jesus on my mind.

MARY

He taught me how to cleanse myself
Of the dirt within my life.
Of hanging out in unclean places
And starting fights with knives

Of running from the police vans
On MacArthur Boulevard
From smoking crack
And getting drunk
From smoking crack
And getting drunk

MARTHA, MARY, and CHORUS

I got the Holy Spirit on my mind
I got the Holy Spirit on my mind
I got myself together
I was delivered by the Lord
Jesus. Jesus.
I got Jesus on my mind.

*(Some of the PARK PEOPLE approach MARY. They embrace
her and begin to talk to her. We don't hear them. Spotlight on
ANNE, who sings while issuing soup. Mainly Rap.)*

ANNE

Yes. But . . .
Has she left the grime of her life?
A life so ugly and sordid
My daughter
Who behaves like a boarder.
She's never home
She's fond of disorder.
She's a curse upon our household.
The devil inhabits her mouth.

And now these strange men
Her friends
They quit their jobs
To tend the sick.
Fishermen make good money, too.
Tricks?
Does she still need a fix?
Says she gave it up for Jesus
But still I wonder
Is he God's son?
Lazarus was my son.
This Jesus has brought him back.
Oh, did I cry so.
I did not want him to die.
Will he die again?
He was a beautiful young boy.
Talented, smart, he was such a joy

But he came home sick one day.
He began to waste away.
In bed for months he lay.
His death made us grieve
They say that it's a miracle.
They don't have to wait on him
Hand and foot.
They don't have to clean his mess,
These men.
                    (Tearful)
Their hearts don't fly out of them

When they look at him.
Only a mother can express that.
Only a mother.
He wasn't meant to be brought back.
It's not right to bring back the dead.
It's not right to bring back the dead.

He's never been the same since he
Came from the tomb.
Sometimes I wish he'd never
Come from my womb.

MARTHA
(From her position at the food table. To ANNE)
At least he's alive, Mother.

ANNE
(A cappella: To MARTHA)
You call this alive?
(ANNE points to LAZARUS, who has been sitting in the park.
He wears a hooded robe and has been staring at the floor. He
slowly rises and faces the audience. He looks emaciated and
coughs while singing his song.)

CHORUS
Lazarus. Lazarus.

LAZARUS

(*To audience*)

I live among the dead and the undead.
One side bliss, the other side dread.
One hand in God's hand
One foot on the floor.
I am pulled through one door
    But part of me
    Remains on the other side
    Of the door.

    I was sleeping deeply
A sleep divine
When the sun shocked my eyes.
I heard the cries
Of my sisters
I heard the cries
Of my mother
I walked out of the cave
And Jesus was
Weeping in his white robe
No bleach in the world
Could make such a white robe
And Jesus said:

He said come forth Lazarus
He said come forth Lazarus
He said come forth Lazarus

CHORUS

He said come forth Lazarus
He said come forth Lazarus
He said come forth Lazarus
  Glory Allelujah
   A miracle. A miracle.
Glory Allelujah.

CHORUS	LAZARUS
	(Interworked with CHORUS)
He said come forth Lazarus	My mother embraced me
He said come forth Lazarus	Mary anointed me
He said come forth Lazarus	The crowd was applauding
Glory Allelujah	
A miracle. A miracle.	
Glory Allelujah.	

LAZARUS and CHORUS

They said:
  Allelujah
  Allelujah Allelujah
A miracle. A miracle. *(Repeat stanza 2 times)*

LAZARUS

I live in the world of the dead
And I live in the world of the undead
But no one
Not even my mother
Can understand

My cries
For how can you return
        To your daily grind
When you had a glimpse of
Paradise

I live between two worlds
Between the night and the day
        I don't know whether to go
        Or whether to stay
    (LAZURUS returns to sitting position, head down again.)

ANNE

He was a good child like
You, Martha.
                (To audience)
Martha is like me
Likes children.
A homemaker. A devoted daughter.
A wonderful baker.
You should taste her cakes
She was delivering food
To this very park
When she was caught in the crossfire
Of some Uzi-shooting hoods.
She thinks that Jesus can cure her
But look what he did to Lazarus
He just broods and broods

MARTHA and TRIO
(*To ANNE*)

Where's your faith my mother?

MARTHA and CHORUS

In works most wondrous and strange
Our Lord is healing my brother
And He will make me walk again
                    (*Spotlight on PETER*)
Walk Walk Walk Walk again
Walk Walk Walk Walk again
And He will make me walk again

PETER

I had a dream so weird last night
Of Beelzebub and his crew
They were taunting Mary Magdalene
They were giving her the blues
They were giving her the blues

Her faith I think is wavering
Her love for Christ is weak, I fear
You cannot trust her word
'Cause she's made of desire and tears
(You know how women are)

JOHN

He said that *you'd* betray him
When the cock crows three times

JAMES

He doubts our steadfast faith in him
He speaks of omens and signs

PETER

It's all this strain and traveling
He hasn't slept in days

(Spoken)

He hasn't had a chance to think.

(Sung)

Ignore him when he says
That we will all abandon him
That we will sell him out
Our love for him is firm and true
Of that there is no doubt

JUDAS

(To audience)

That Peter
His weapon is surer than his words.
He is not of keen intelligence.
Only with the tongue of God
Will he teach with eloquence.
He thinks his sword will
Dissuade Rome
He thinks that Jesus
Is from above
Jesus—a man of shifting moods
But a man whom I love.

JAMES and JOHN

We were mending our nets
When we answered his call
He blew into town like a
Gentle squall
We will be with him
Till his fall

PETER

I was fishing for cod
When I came under the sway of the Lord
His words
As sweet as a bluejay's song

JOHN, JAMES, and PETER

I will never desert him
I will always be with him
We will all be with him till his fall
We will all be with him till his fall
Till his fall.

JUDAS

(To audience)

They gave him their word. These men
He doesn't trust them.
He rebukes and scolds them
At every turn
And spurns their pleas of love
These simple men they're not like me

No questions snare these brothers
Oh, how did I become involved
With this?
I did not join like the others
I did not come from Galilee
Galilee. A place of fanatics.
Galilee. A place of lost causes.
Am I the only clear-minded one?
I'm not from Galilee.
I'm from Ker-ri-oth. Keee-ri-oth.
On the other hand
He's saying things that
Need to be said
                    (Preaches)
        About the Pharisees.
        About this Jew hater Pilate
        About what is going on in the temple.
        About water carriers using it as a shortcut.
        About the rich paying for sacrifices
        Those animals screaming in agony
        Day and night at the temple.

            JUDAS, PETER, JOHN, and JAMES
Cattle sellers
Sheep sellers
Pigeon sellers
Playing cards
Laughing
Laughing

Laughing
Laughing

JUDAS

Laughing,
Playing cards.
I used to be with them
Hanging out in rock houses
Morning, noon, and night
That's before I met my Jesus
Now I'm doing right

JOHN, JAMES, and CHORUS

If we did not believe in him
Why would we have
Joined his cause
And stood with him
When he defied their laws
And stood with him
When he trashed their bank
And stood with him against
The mob so rank

PETER, JAMES, and JOHN

If we were not worthy
Why would we risk our lives
Our careers
Stood against the taxpayers' curses
Stood against their taunts and jeers

PETER

And now he decides to pray.
When he was warned
That he should not tarry
That Pilate was waiting
For the chance to arrest him.
That Beelzebub is eager
To torture and test him
I will never shun.
This Jesus, God's son.
I'm ready for trouble,
I've got myself a gun
Got myself a gun.

(DISCIPLES enter the park)

DISCIPLES

You may have a chance
To use it

JAMES

What can this mean?

JOHN

What can this mean?

PETER

There may be strife.

DISCIPLES

There's a plot under way
To take Jesus' life

We came to the park
As soon as we heard

As soon as this patrolman
Gave us the word
He said, "Jesus, your Lord."
He said, "Jesus, your Lord."

HIGHWAY PATROLMAN

This Jesus your Lord
I owe him one
He saved my servant
From a life undone
I overheard Governor Pilate
Who has a short fuse.
He wants to murder Jesus
And blame it on the Jews.

Among the right-wing governors
He is the one who is most shrewd.
Says he knows all the tactics for
Dealing with fanatics

JOHN, PETER, and JAMES

Why Jesus?

HIGHWAY PATROLMAN

They've been watching Jesus
Since he came into town
Governor Pilate says too many people are
Gathering around
He said that a man who
Draws so many people
Is dangerous
To roam the streets
Is scandalous

PETER

Hurry, we must warn him
            (They begin to exit. JUDAS remains.)

JAMES

Hurry, we must warn him

JOHN

Hurry, we must warn him

PETER

Judas, you coming?

JUDAS

No. I have to make a run into town.
You need anything?

PETER

Be careful.
Be careful.
Be careful.

ACT 1
Scene 2

CHORUS

Our God is in the heavens
He does whatever He pleases
Our God is in the heavens
He does what pleases Him
Their idols are silver and gold
From the work of men's hands
They are molds.
They have mouths
But do not speak
Eyes, but do not see
They have ears but do not hear
Noses, but do not smell
They have hands but do not feel
Feet, but do not walk
And they do not make a sound
In their throat

Those who make them are like
Them
So are all who trust in them

TESTIFYING WOMAN

I want to testify
I say I want to testify
About what Jesus has done for me
I ain't tellin' you no lie
To anyone with ears to hear
To anyone with eyes to see
My daughter was one of those
Victims
The devil chose to seize
We were among the first in line
When Jesus came that day
His men would not let us through
Told us to go away

CHORUS

Amen Sister, tell the story

TESTIFYING WOMAN

They said he could not see
Us
They said that we were bums
That I and my child weren't
Nothin' but mangy dogs
And not His favored ones

I said Lord, we're not askin' for
The table
Just hand us some of the crumbs
I said, "Lord, we're not askin' for
The table
Just hand us some of the crumbs"
And Jesus said,
"So great is your faith
That you will have your will."
And when he said that
Oh brothers and sisters
My little baby was
Healed

CHORUS

To anyone with ears to hear
To anyone with eyes to see
I want to testify
I want to testify
To anyone with ears to hear
To anyone with eyes to see
I want to testify
What Jesus has done for me
What Jesus has done for me

Our God is in the heavens
He does whatever He pleases
Our God is in the heavens
He does whatever He pleases

God is in His heavens
God is in His heavens
God is in His heavens
He does what pleases Him *(Repeat 4 times)*

God is in His heavens
He does what pleases Him

Act 2
Scene 1

CHORUS

We are the despised
The convicted, the evicted
We are convicted, indicted, evicted
We are the people of
Gethsemane Park

When we die
When we die
We are taken out with trash
Didn't anybody listen to the Lord?
Or are you too busy making cash?
Didn't anybody listen to the Lord?

MARTHA

Jesus said,
"Truly I say unto you
As you would do to one of

The least of these
You did it to me,
You did it to me too."

CHORUS

"For when I was hungry
You gave me no food
When I was thirsty, you gave me
No drink
I was a stranger
You did not welcome me
I was sick. I was sick and you did
Not visit me."
Didn't anybody listen to the Lord?
Just take it from the man from Galilee.
Didn't anybody listen to the Lord?

CHILDREN

We are the children of Gethsemane
Park
We've never seen the ocean
We've never seen a lark.
Our fathers are dead or driven to drink.
Our mothers' minds are at the brink.
Our days are spent panhandling
Most of us wish we'd never been born
We are the children of Gethsemane Park.

We are the despised
We are the convicted.

We are convicted, indicted, evicted
We are the people of Gethsemane Park.

MARTHA

Jesus said
Whoever shall receive one
Child in my name
Receives me
For whoever gives you a
Glass of water
Shall not lose his reward
And whoever
Offends Christ's children

(BEELZEBUB and 3 ASSOCIATES enter with 6 TAXPAYERS
[3 WOMEN and 3 MEN]. The WOMEN are dressed in red.
The MEN wear pin-striped suits and blue and red ties.)

MALE TAXPAYER
(To BEELZEBUB)
Can't you do something about these people?

OTHERS

Yeh, yeh, yeh.

BEELZEBUB and ASSOCIATES
(Sly, obsequious)
We're doing our utmost to make an arrest
But waiting for evidence is always the best

We need an eyewitness to identify this pest
He'll be out of your hair in no time
No less
If it were up to Pilate
They'd all be gone
Interrogated, tortured, crucified, and done
But his hands are tied by the people in Rome
He'll capture this Christ
And make him an example

FEMALE TAXPAYER
(Noticing MARTHA and ANNE)

Martha, Anne what are you doing with
These people? You live in the hills like us.
Why are you betraying your own kind
Wasting precious time serving soup lines?

ANNE

I'm helping my daughter. Jesus raised
Lazarus. She thinks that he can help her.
(ANNE shrugs her shoulders)

MARTHA
(To TAXPAYER)

Render unto Caesar that which
Is Caesar's but render unto God
That which is God's
The park belongs to God
The air belongs to God
Your taxes can't buy grasses

Or squirrels or flowers or trees
The love of God can't be entered
By the recorder of the deeds

TAXPAYER
(To BEELZEBUB)

Excuses. Excuses
Is there no end to your incompetence?
Your insufferable impenitence?
We pay our taxes and look what we get
Our park overtaken by derelicts
Thieves and robbers, an accursed lot
Drunkards and crazies and
Runaways smoking pot
Gays and lesbians
And every possible transgressor

(Turns to PARK PEOPLE)

We're tired of you and your
Filthy band
Creating chaos in our
Stable land
Making protests with no
Good reason
At the height of our busiest tourist
Season
You're giving us crowd control
Problems

AFDC CHILDREN
(To TAXPAYERS)

CHILD #1

Could you live on $240 per month?

CHILD #2

My family does

CHILD #3

Could you live without indoor plumbing?

CHILD #1

My family does

CHILD #2

Could you share your bed with rats?

CHILD #3

We do

CHILD #3

Would you cover your toothache with cotton?

CHILD #2

I do

CHILD #1

Could your children do their homework in a shelter?

ALL 3

We do

TAXPAYERS' LEAGUE

Why don't you take a bath?
Oh. Why don't you cut your hair?
Tell me why can't you find some work?
Why are you so much of a bother?
Where's your father?

BEELZEBUB, ASSOCIATES, and TAXPAYERS
(Shrilly)

Hey!

(BEELZEBUB approaches JOHN)

BEELZEBUB

Let me see some I.D. *(Repeat 3 times)*
Where you come from? *(Repeat 4 times)*

JOHN

I came up from Mexico
Crossed the border during the night
I came up from Mexico
Crossed the border during the night
Want to make a better life for
My children and my wife
Want to make a better life for
My children and my wife
(Spoken)
I make the beds and scrub the floors
In the motel on the freeway
All for the sake of my children
May they have a better day

TAXPAYERS
(Spoken)

These people are like animals in a pound
They've taken over our beautiful downtown
Everywhere their children are bound
In ragged shoes and tattered gowns

Urinating in public places
Begging for food and places to sleep
We need more policemen on the street
                    (Sung)
Move them out they're taking up space!

WOMAN #1

You want us out of sight
And out of mind
But we won't go away
Our numbers grow in the cities,
The census people say.

MAN #1

Your leaders cut our benefits
They punish us with jail

WOMAN #2

Our lives are lived in misery

MAN #2

In this other side of Hell

MARY MAGDALENE

But Jesus gave us soulful words
That you had better rue
He does not take the side of Kings
He said, "I'm the least of you."

CHORUS *(Verse 1)*

He said, "I am the least of you."
He said, "I am the least of you."

PETER

He didn't say, "I own the finest car in town."

MARY MAGDALENE

Or, "I've got pearls in a gold crown."

CHORUS

He said, "I am the least of you."

CHORUS *(Verse 2)*

He said, "I am the least of you."
He said, "I am the least of you."

MARTHA

He didn't say, "I score the highest on every test."

JOHN

Or, "I am handsomer than all the rest."

CHORUS

He said, "I am the least of you."
            (Drive) He said, I I I I I I I (4 times)
He said, "I am the least of you."

*(MARY the MOTHER enters, all out of breath. BEELZEBUB
and ASSOCIATES move toward her. TAXPAYERS are sur-
prised. PARK PEOPLE bow.)*

MARY

(Moves toward BEELZEBUB and 3 ASSOCIATES)

You want to kill my baby

Hunt him down like a tramp

What is he guilty of?

What has he done?

Has he killed someone?

CHORUS

Not That We Know Of

MARY

Is he a thief?

CHORUS

Not That We Know Of

MARY

Has he preached against the state?

CHORUS

Not That We Know Of

MARY

Has he run off with somebody's wife?

CHORUS

Not That We Know Of

MARY

Has he taken somebody's life?

CHORUS

Not That We Know Of

CHORUS and MARY

For raising the dead, he's guilty
For feeding the poor, he's guilty
For making the lame straight, he's guilty
For speaking his heart and for healing my soul. . .
Guilty, guilty as charged.

BEELZEBUB

Don't listen to her
Look at the sky
The moon doesn't look right
Listen to the streets
Madly the dogs are barking
Listen to the birds
They seem to be quarreling
The man's a witch
And he's left you in the ditch
Where is he now that you're in trouble
Probably skipped town on the double
    (BEELZEBUB, TAXPAYER, TAXPAYERS laugh. JOHN,
        ANDREW, and JAMES nod.)

AFDC CHILD

Jesus hasn't left us
He's with us in this park

ALL CHILDREN

Jesus hasn't left us

(MARTHA joins)

He's with us in the park.

CHORUS

For eyes that can see
And for ears that can hear

MALE TAXPAYER
(Sarcastically)

If the man is in residence
Show us some evidence

CHORUS

Jesus hasn't left us
He's here inside the park
Jesus hasn't left us
He's here inside the park

For eyes that can see
And for ears that can hear

Jesus hasn't left us
He's here inside the park
Jesus hasn't left us
He's here inside the park

CHILDREN

Jesus hasn't left us.
Jesus hasn't left us. (*Repeat 2 times*)

ALL

Jesus hasn't left us. (*Many times*)
Jesus hasn't left us. He's here inside my heart.

CHILD
(*Spoken*)

Show us a sign, Jesus

(*MARTHA begins to struggle to stand up from her wheel-
chair. Shock sweeps the faces of BEELZEBUB, DEMON
ASSOCIATES, and TAXPAYERS. She struggles to the center
of the stage, getting stronger with every step. She finally
breaks into a Pentecostal holiness dance, while PEOPLE'S
CHORUS clap hands and play tambourines. She dances
toward BEELZEBUB'S ASSOCIATES. The CHORUS and 3
TAXPAYERS flee the stage. Others join MARTHA until every-
body is dancing, 3 TAXPAYERS who are left behind drop to
their knees in a prayerlike pose. CURTAIN.*)

ACT 2
Scene 2

(*Spotlight on BEELZEBUB and ASSOCIATES*)

BEELZEBUB

My associates and I
Are in the cold. Woe. Woe.

ASSOCIATES

We travel through unclean places
Seeking hosts to hold.
He turned our brothers into pigs
And drowned them in the sea.

BEELZEBUB

This all happened at Gerasenes

BEELZEBUB and ASSOCIATES

We wished he'd remained in Galilee.
We wished he'd remained in Galilee.

> *(Howl. Howl.)*

FIRST ASSOCIATE

This Jesus is messing with business
He's giving evil a bad name
He's taking all of our customers
He's putting us out of the souls game

BEELZEBUB

How do I get to Jesus
I've tried everything
In the book
Offered him

Gold diamonds and women
The son of God is not
A crook

BEELZEBUB and ASSOCIATES

A rumor's afoot
That he's working for us
A rumor that we'll nurture and
Encourage.
We'll work through his enemies
We'll work as his scourge
He'll meet his end at Gethsemane.
He will be through in Gethsemane.

(ASSOCIATE enters, shoving JUDAS)

ASSOCIATE

Look what I found.

BEELZEBUB

Isn't that one of Christ's men?

ASSOCIATE

Judas. We caught him at a crack house.

BEELZEBUB

I thought that you were saved, Judas?

ASSOCIATES
(Sarcastically)

Turned over a new leaf

BEELZEBUB

What happened to your 12-step program?
(ASSOCIATES and BEELZEBUB laugh)
Your faith is weak
Your doubts are strong
You don't know what's right
You don't know what is wrong
I'll win you over
At the very end

BEELZEBUB and ASSOCIATES
(Encircling JUDAS)

What is your mission?
What is your quest?
Are you the actor
In a holy test?
Are you to follow him
To the very end?
Do you betray him?
Do you turn him in?
Is it all planned?
Or is it all chance?
Is it God's fate?
And is it too late?

BEELZEBUB

These are the questions
That rob your sleep
That worry your soul
You cannot eat
You cannot keep

ASSOCIATES

Beelzebub at bay

JUDAS

I had a relapse. Can't you give me something?

BEELZEBUB

Oh, he wants us to give him something.
(BEELZEBUB and ASSOCIATES laugh)

BEELZEBUB
(Holds up crack bag)

I got it right here.

(JUDAS reaches for it and BEELZEBUB taunts him by
offering it to him then pulling it away. JUDAS drops to his
knees)

JUDAS

Please. I beseech you.

BEELZEBUB

It's yours.

JUDAS

Thank you.
> (*Drops to his knees and hugs BEELZEBUB's leg*)

BEELZEBUB

But there's one condition.

JUDAS

Anything. Anything.

BEELZEBUB

We return to Gethsemane Park and you
identify this Messiah. You do that. We'll
Give you all of the rock that you can use.
> (*BEELZEBUB and ASSOCIATES laugh.*)

Deal?
> (*JUDAS nods. BEELZEBUB grabs JUDAS by the hair.*)

ASSOCIATES

Deal. Deal. Deal. Deal.
> (*JUDAS nods*)

BEELZEBUB

Future generations
Will thank you.
> (*BEELZEBUB and ASSOCIATES laugh*)

Okay, men, lets move out.

> (ASSOCIATES and BEELZEBUB prepare to depart for
> Gethsemane Park)

JUDAS

(Sings to the audience)

When the unclean spirit
Has gone out of a man
It passes through waterless
Places seeking rest
But It finds none
Then It says
I will return to my house
From which I came
And when It comes
It finds the house empty
Swept
And put in order
Then It goes and brings
With It
Seven other spirits
More evil than itself
And they enter and
Dwell there
And the last state of a
Man becomes worse than
The first
Unclean spirit. Unclean spirit. Ah.

*(JUDAS begins to weep. ASSOCIATES exit, with one of the
ASSOCIATES pushing JUDAS.)*

ACT 2
Scene 3

TESTIFYING WOMAN *(A cappella)*

Stay away Friday, I don't want

This day to go

Stay away Friday, I don't want

This day to go

Tomorrow they're going

To hang him

This man I love him

So

Oh, stay away Friday. Stay away.

So stay away Friday, stay away

*(Repeat stanza 2 times. 2nd time CHORUS [a cappella / feet
stamp on 1st and 3rd beats])*

MOTHER MARY

They'll take him from this garden

With ropes around his hands

They'll take him from this garden

With ropes around his hands

A follower will betray him

And feed him to the damned

MARTHA

They'll pierce his side with daggers

Till blood runs down his side
They'll pierce his side with daggers
Till blood runs down his side
They'll torture him and taunt him
Until his life subsides

MARY MAGDALENE

Please don't kill my Jesus
Don't take him away from me
Please don't kill my Jesus
Don't take him away from me
He never beat or cursed me
He made my demons flee
Oh, stay away Friday. Stay away.

MARY MAGDALENE, MARY MOTHER, MARTHA, and
CHORUS

Stay away Friday, oh *(Repeat 8 times)*
Stay away Friday. Stay away.
 *(The two MARYs and MARTHA embrace. BEELZEBUB
 enters with JUDAS. JOHN, JAMES, PETER, and other
 DISCIPLES flee.)*

BEELZEBUB
(To JUDAS)

Point out Jesus the troublemaker
And you'll get all of the smoke
That you need.

CHORUS

Don't do it, Judas. Don't do it.
Your name will be stained
For all time to come
Take your time, Judas
Take your time, Judas

BEELZEBUB

Point him out, Judas, and
We will make you rich

CHORUS

Take your time, Judas
Take your time

BEELZEBUB

Identify him, Judas
Identify this witch

CHORUS

Take your time, Judas
Take your time, Judas.
Take your time.
Take your time.

BEELZEBUB
(*To CHORUS*)

Shut up!

DISCIPLES

Judas, don't listen to them
Judas, stand your ground
Don't turn the Lord over
To His enemies

BEELZEBUB

Judas, Judas, you want that rock, don't you?
Show us this man
Reveal this demon
With a kiss
(*JUDAS hesitates and then begins to kiss the PARK PEOPLE,*
one at a time.)

CHORUS and DISCIPLES

Blessed. Blessed (*Repeat 5 times*)
Blessed are the poor in spirit,
For theirs is the kingdom of heaven,
Oh, blessed are those who mourn,
For they shall be comforted
Blessed are the meek,
For they shall inherit the earth,
And blessed are those who hunger and thirst for righteousness,
For they shall obtain mercy.

BEELZEBUB

(*Frustrated, furious*)
If they want to play hardball

We can do that too
I'll torture every one of them
We'll beat them black and blue
Until they tell us which one
Is the Galilean son

                    CHORUS
Blessed.

                    BEELZEBUB
And when we capture Jesus
Our work will be finally done
To getting into people's heads
Making them howl all night in
Cemeteries, and bruising themselves

                    CHORUS
Blessed are the pure in heart, for they shall see
God
                    BEELZEBUB
Associates, come out!
Associates, come out!
I order you to possess these people
    (*Turns to the PARK PEOPLE who are on their knees praying
                        and singing*)
Ha. Looks like Jesus has deserted you.
Associates come out!!

MARY MAGDALENE

Jesus, don't let them bind us
Show us a sign!

(Suddenly, while the PEOPLE onstage are singing, we hear the grunts and oinks of PIGS off-stage. ASSOCIATES have been converted into swine and, wearing pig masks, enter the stage and romp about aimlessly. Shocked and frightened, BEELZEBUB convulses and is also transformed into a pig. The pigs leave the stage and run up the aisle of the theater oinking, squealing, and grunting away.)

CHORUS

We are
Blessed. Blessed. *(Repeat 3 times)*
Blessed are the peacemakers
For they shall be called the children of God.

Blessed. Blessed. *(3 times)*
Blessed are the peacemakers,
For they shall be called the children of God.

Blessed. Blessed. *(3 times)*
Blessed are the peacemakers,
For they shall be called the children of God.

(CURTAIN)

SNAKE WAR

Snake War

(Based upon chapter VIII of D. O. Fagunwa's *Igbo Olodu-mare* [The Forest of God], "Ojola-Ibinu Ti Ise Olori Ejo Aiye Gbogbo" or "Ojola-Ibinu, the King of Snakes everywhere")

Some hunters are lost in Igbo Olodumare; they find refuge in the home of Baba-onirungbon-yeuke.

Baba-onirungbon-yeuke was a wonderful host to those of us hunters who were stranded in the Igbo Olodumare. He provided us with all of the comforts of forest living.

We would bring wild boar to him and he would cook it for us. He prepared yams for us that were as crispy as those one would find in a Thai restaurant. At night, the forest women would dance for us and perform on their instruments. We swam in pools that had escaped man's invasion. We avoided coffee and strived on green tea. All of us, who were in our middle age were beginning to feel many years younger. Why, he said, would we want to return to the city and its crime, pollution, noise and other corruptions? Women, who, unlike these forest ones, were only interested in using a man as a pack mule to buy them jewelry, cars and clothes. He did not have a kind view of city women. Said they were addicted to airport novels and getting their nails done and shopping for weaves.

He invited us to stay there with him in the forest. We could grow our own food, hunt and make our own clothes and provide for our own entertainment, sparing us the music and films of carnality so rife in the urban areas. The forest, he said, not only provides man's needs but is a great teacher, a great university. But we told him that we had been away from our families for months and that we had to return to the city to meet our responsibilities. He was of course disappointed but said that he would help us find our way back home. With this remark we discovered that he knew more than he had let on. And that in these forests of beautiful women, birds and animals, this hunter was lonely for the company of men. This is why he had done everything possible to prolong our stay.

He entered his study of secret books and returned with a map, which he spread out on the table. He pointed to our city, which was about one hundred miles from the forest, but warned us that we would have to traverse some dangerous territory before we arrived there. One place was marked the City of Strange Birds, another was the City of Venomous Worms and the most dangerous of all, the City of Snakes, ruled by the most feared animal on earth, *Ojola-ibinu ti ise olori ejo aiye gbogbo*. If we could make our way through this city, then we'd have no problems with the worms and the birds, some of which were one hundred years old.

Obviously Baba-onirungbon-yeuke cared a lot about us. He went to his safe and opened it. But instead of returning with money he brought back what looked like an ordinary bottle of water. He said that if we ever had any difficulty, the water would be of help to us. He told us that the water was from a river that flows through heaven. No one is capable of collecting a portion of the water except those who live there. But Baba was able to collect some of this water as a favor from his friend Iku (who is Baron Samedi in Haiti and Guede in Miami and Brooklyn, eniti ile re mbe lagbedemeji aiye on orun = the entity that dwells between heaven and earth). He said that without his help he would not have been able to collect the water.

He said that in order to collect the water he had to borrow garments that dead people put on before they can enter into heaven. Attired in these clothes, he arrived at the strange river that flows through heaven. Iku had instructed him that anyone who wished to collect this water in heaven must not look at it when he collects it. He must turn his back on it. The reason is that the person must not plainly see the throne of Olorun Oba and heavenly spirits who surround his throne; spirits who praise their creator who created us all. The person who saw the holy ones who are around the throne of God would see an incredibly beautiful sight. But the person who sees the shadow of Olorun Oba sees the evil side. The person who discovers the dwelling side of the creator's shadow might be damned through the generations.

Baba said that he had followed Iku's instructions to a T and that indeed the strange water in the bottle had magical properties. If one should pour it on top of plants and command the plants to turn into people, it will be done. If one would say that the plant should become an animal, it will become an animal because Olorun Oba, acting through the water, would command it to become that animal. Baba instructed us on how to use it. He said when you use this water, you must not taste of palm oil, you must not taste of salt and you must not taste of pepper; you must be completely naked, just as you came into the world and just as you will return to heaven. Everybody thanked this Ologbon profusely. Baba, the red bearded gentleman who lives at the top of the rock. He cares very much for humanity. He really took care of us. None of us ever mocked the old school again.

On the morning of the second day, we left the house, I almost cried because I had nothing to give to Baba's family. When I looked inside my bag, I had about ten dollars to my name. I was ashamed to give this to his children as a present. When I again looked inside my bag I saw some cake that my mother gave me the other day when she brought the cake and collard greens from heaven. The day that she wanted to buoy my sagging spirits. I shared it with them, but this too for me was insufficient. The others of my party also presented gifts as thanks for all the care that he showed to us. He refused the gifts. They were not important to him. He is one of those people who does not expect people to pay him in return for his kindness. He is a man whose hopes are with Olorun Oba.

Many people are simply vain. When some people show kindness they have the expectation that the recipient of this kindness knows about it. Such a person leans on the

thin air. Baba gives anonymously. He does not strut about,
boasting that he has extended his beneficence to this
person or that person. He is not like those human beings
who seek to harvest yams where they have not planted
yams, people who expect bananas where they have not
planted bananas.

When Baba finished, Ijambaforiti rose, and he said, "Com-
rades, look at me closely; I am Ijam the elephant killer. I
have proven that I am not afraid of death. I am not afraid
of sickness. I do not suffer grief in the afternoon; I do not
experience restlessness at night. I ask all of you today, can
a person lead others without that person having done
something big before? An elephant killer? A person who
does not walk in fear? A person who is alive. Therefore, we
must go." He turned to Baba. "My dear friend, I thank you
for your past caring. This is what I want you to do for us. I
want you to give us a clear direction of the way home. God
willing, by tomorrow we will not be here in this house. It
is mandatory that we leave."

After what Ijam said everybody was silent. I arose. I
supported him. When I sat down, Olohun-duru rose and
began to speak; his voice was so sweet that when he sat
down Baba said to him, "Olodumare has strewn your lips
with sweetness." When he was convinced we were leaving,
Baba decided to assist us to the best of his ability. He took
out a trumpet and showed it to us and asked if there was
any one of us who could play the instrument. Olohun-duru
replied that he could blow it very well. Baba gave the

trumpet to Olohun-duru and told him that when he approached the snake village to begin to blow it and when the snake policeman who watched the highway heard the sounds they would go to sleep.

He said that the snake policeman who watched the highway is the meanest and if they pass by this snake their troubles would be over unless they did not follow everything that he said to them.

He instructed that they must not kill a snake in the city—he emphasized this. He said that the person who killed a snake in the city will see a snake war. He said that when we arrive at this city we will encounter a variety of snakes. It's a snake market place where things that are delicious to snakes are on sale. White mice. Rabbits. They roam around this marketplace selling and buying merchandise.

He said that Ojola-ibinu is the King of the Snake City. He is a creature who is angrier than any of the creatures who move about on their bellies. He stressed again that killing a snake would lead to much trouble. He said that we'd be dragged before this terrible king and possibly eaten. After this, Baba gave a large gourd to Ewedaiyepo. The gourd's body was black like that of a snake. Around its neck were bird feathers. Baba told Ewedaiyepo that the gourd contained an antidote and that we must take a spoonful daily until we arrived home. If we did this the snake poison will not affect us, he said.

When we left Baba (eniti ngbe ibi gegele okuta), we experienced a lot of things on the path. Given the things we experienced directly and the things that we experienced indirectly—had it not been that God is great, I myself would not have been able to speak today.

On the afternoon of the second day, after we left Baba, around 3 o'clock, we arrived near the City of Snakes ruled by Ojola-ibinu. A iittle before we arrived at the city we began to hear the frightened sounds of various birds and squirrels. When we appeared on the highway, we saw the snake policemen straight in front of us. They were looking in our direction. I was so afraid the string of my trousers became loose. What surprised me most was that the snake policemen resembled people. Their heads were those of persons but their bodies were those of snakes. They had a pair of short feet, with which they walked very well. Their tails were long and their bodies were covered with scales. There wasn't one of them who wasn't as big as a man. They were indeed terrible looking.

Olohun-duru began to blow his trumpet, and the snakes, after twisting about in ecstasy, became still. They were asleep. We tiptoed over them, careful not to make a noise or cause a disturbance. But I regret that it was here that one member of our party, Aguntan-inaki, lost his life. When we arose that morning, we began to take the antidote that Baba gave us. The antidote that would protect us from snakebite. It was very bitter. So bitter that Aguntan didn't want to take it. And so when we were leaving the place of the snake police, then asleep, Aguntan wanted to use the bathroom; we waited for him to finish, and when he didn't finish quickly we started to walk ahead of him.

As Aguntan was about to catch up with us, he began to make noise; he was shouting; his voice filled the hollows of the forest. He was shouting, "Wait. Wait up!" The snake police awoke and bit him immediately. The poison took effect, and within seconds his life was ended. Although Aguntan was a foolish person, we all cried. All except Ijambaforiti. He did not cry. He began to whistle and sing a parable. He said that by being so careless and thoughtless in making noise, Aguntan could well have exposed us. From that day on if a child refuses to take medicine we called that child Aguntan-inaki.

We increased our pace of walking; while the snake police were busy disposing of Agutan's body, we evaded them. When we left the vicinity of the snake police, we encountered other snakes one by one, but they did not bite us, they went their way.

When we walked a little farther, we started to see fences that the snakes built. Inside these enclosures, they'd collected many toads. They were taking care of them, tending to them as one would a goat. These fat toads were food for their guests, who'd come from all over the world to attend a sort of snake Chautauqua that the dictator Oloibinu arranged for visiting delegations of snakes. They were housed in a five-star snake hotel that had been built near a beach located at the edge of the city. Inside this fence, I plainly saw toads that were as large as cocks. The path through the City of Snakes was smooth and shining; there were many body skins on the ground and heaps of rubbish on the path. As we walked along, snakes dropped down ahead of us. Snakes fell on our shoulders and crawled around our feet. But since we'd drank from the bottle whose contents were drawn from the river that flows near the throne of Olodumare, they could not injure us.

For some reason the snakes seemed curious about Ijam the elephant hunter. One snake started crawling around Ijam, starting from his feet to his shoulder. When it reached his shoulder the snake stopped and did not move. A second snake started crawling around Ijam until he reached the other side of his shoulder. When both snakes saw each other they started to play around Ijam's neck. They would not stop. Ijam remained calm throughout this ordeal, but finally, he tightened his pants. He took his Sango stick. He laughed. Looked at us as powerful people look at others. He said, "People who are ready to die meet those who are ready to kill them. I am the man named Ijam. I accept most things but not insults. A person never dies twice. If death will take me, I'll go."

As he said this, he took both snakes and threw them to the ground; he took his Sango stick and hit on the snakes on the head with the stick until he killed them. Trouble broke out.

As Ijam did this we heard a bell strike. Before we knew it, the snake police ran toward us and started to bite us, but their poison did not take effect because of the medicine that we had taken in the morning of that day. When they saw that nothing happened they took us to the home of the chief of all snakes.

When we came before the head snake my thinking ability returned. I never thought I'd be alive again. Since I have been on earth, I have never seen a creature as awesome as the chief of the snakes. Ojola-ibinu was very large. He was a creeping creature with the head of a man. Except that his mouth was as big as a man's. Sheep are not enough to satisfy Ojola's appetite. When he eats, he usually eats two cows. When we arrived at the King's court, snakes were gathered around his throne; it was a royal state. Every one of his chiefs sat around him. Just as much as the King inspires fear, he is handsome. His body resembled precious stones and diamonds. When he sat, he was like a little hill.

He was very angry. His head turned and started growing large. All of his chiefs began to express impatience with us. They charged us with killing two snake children. Ojola glared at us while the snake was discussing Ijam's crime. When Ojola began to talk, his voice rang out like a threatening rain. His eyes were like red beads. They cried out with anger. He addressed us.

"People of the earth, only God of Glory can end the conflict among us poisonous snakes and people, and non-poisonous snakes and people. When a person sees a snake in the open, he kills it, when a person sees a snake in a closed place, he kills it. There is no enmity like the enmity between snakes and people except the enmity between the children of Satan and the children of God.

"You take these, my snake police. You assemble them in my courtyard. You select the fat one," he said, pointing to Ijam. "You kill him for me. Then fatten the others, I shall eat all of them. Killers end generally in destruction. They who kill my children—I will certainly kill their children. As long as I am alive I will not see human beings and let them go."

When he finished speaking the evil creature burst out laughing while his chiefs sang his praises. "Salutations to the king ruler! Second to the Orisha! You sit wise at the top of mankind! Powerful one at the top! Chief over the stubborn! Death to the disobedient humans!" they said, pointing to us.

After this, we were taken to the rear of the palace. When we arrived we found 25 other hostages. They'd missed their way or got lost in the forest and fell into the hands of the King's snake police. At the end of the courtyard, there were more than a thousand human skulls stacked in neat rows. The snake police lined us up. They inspected us. They felt our buttocks. They examined our chests, to assess the amount of fat there. When they came to me, they took the man who stood next to me, who was a little fatter than I, and they killed him in front of me.

Not long after this, they brought food to us, but I didn't eat the food because I'd heard them arguing and debating inside the kitchen about whether the medicine they put inside the food was sufficient to make us fat. The King's servants spoke in undertones, but I stood close to the wall of the kitchen and I heard what they said.

While my friends ate the food, I ate a piece of bread that my dead mother gave to me. On the second day, all of

the people who came with us became big and fat. Ijam-
baforiti, whose body is usually sound, had become weak,
fat and shining. When I saw this I called my comrades in
secret, I spoke to them about the things that I noticed and
things that I heard. I told them that I had some bread inside
my pocket that is in an inexhaustible supply and I recom-
mended that we eat it.

When it became the afternoon of the second day, the
King's servants again took one of us who was fat and killed
him for the king. It was just a lucky break for Ijambaforiti,
for when they examined him closely they found that he
was not yet fat enough for dinner.

Thus they gave us food at a different time of day, but no
one ate the food. On the third day, they took a person from
among us and killed him for the King's dinner. Luckily he
didn't belong to our group, but we knew that we were at
risk of being eaten next for they were beginning to sus-
pect our having another food supply. We began to make
urgent plans to survive. We decided that we must kill
Ojola himself. Enia made a suggestion. He noticed that
the creeping creature crawled to his bath every day at
about six o'clock in the morning. It was Ewe's opinion
that if we could collect our machetes we could kill or at
least disable the King of all Snakes. But how would we col-
lect them? The snake police had confiscated our weapons
and locked them up. Ewe said he'd struck up a friendship
with one of the kitchen workers. He was a toad with a
genetic disposition toward a rapid metabolism and so the
snakes were unable to fatten him to feed to their guests. He

and toads like him were assigned to kitchen work. Washing dishes and mopping floors. He was getting on in age and his waistline was beginning to expand. The snake police were beginning to smack their lips as they noticed this. He knew that it wouldn't be long before he'd be served up to visiting delegations of snakes who were arriving to pay their respects to the King of Snakes. From the world over. Except for Anacondas. Anacondas had been feuding with Ojola ever since he was quoted in the *Snake Digest* as ridiculing Anacondas as little more than overgrown worms and for selling out to Hollywood. He called them chumps for doing all of the work while the human actors had great palaces in Beverly Hills and thousands of miles of frequent-flyer miles while they were still crawling around the swamps of the Amazon an endangered species. Noticing that my companions and I were not taking on weight, he'd asked for our diet. We began to give him the sacred corn bread, my mother said was from the cook of all cooks: Vertamae Grosvenor. He was so grateful for our help in staving off his rapid weight gain that he gave us the keys to the cabinet where our captors locked our weapons. We were in business.

When we collected our machetes in the evening, we planted them on the ground, face upwards, in the open. The idea was that when Ojola goes to bathe he would cross over the machetes, and the machete would cut him and split his bosom and his intestines would spill out into the streets. We thanked Ewe and decided to follow his opinion. The toad gave Ewe the key to the storage room where our weapons had been placed. While the snake guards were having their supper Ewe stole to the storage room and liberated our weapons. Ewe collected the machetes and sharpened them. They became as sharp as razors. We put the machetes, turned upward, in the pathway of Ojola. After this, we packed our belongings and prepared to escape amidst all of the chaos surrounding Ojola's murder. On the morning of the second day, very early, Ojola-ibinu was unaware that this was a day that Olodumare would assert his existence. When he came upon the sharp machetes the machetes started to cut him and he began to run forward and the machetes started cutting his stomach; when that happened Ojola screamed (so much so that the inhabitants of the city woke up). The creature struggled, but when he did this his intestines came out on the ground and the earth was full of blood.

There was a great uproar among the snakes. Before he died, he knew that we were responsible. He raged at heaven. He called out curses. He blasphemed Olodumare. His liver and his stomach joined his intestines in the street.

May God never let this kind of thing happen to us. We knew that we, having killed the chief snake, had invited trouble. Informed of their king's death many snakes surrounded the palace. They knew that we'd killed the King. His servants, his spouses and his children who dwelled in the palace came out. As we were about to head out of the city, some of the snakes spotted us and gave chase. They chased us to the end of the city where there was located a snake hotel on the beach. The hotel was hosting a snake convention attended by snakes from all over the world, except the Anacondas who were boycotting Snake City. Most of them were seniors and most of them were asleep having just heard a lecture by a snake professor entitled" "Herpetological Kinetics in D. H. Lawrence's 'The Snake'." They were from all over the world. They awoke to panic horns that were blowing and blasting steam whistles. From North America, there were Eastern coral snakes, Western diamondback rattlesnakes, from South America there were Tropical chicken snakes, Bushmaster snakes, from Europe there were Ursini's vipers, and from Africa Black mambas and Gaboon vipers, and from Asia Green tree pythons and Sea Krait, and from Australia death adders. They joined the snakes from Snake City.

We called out to Olodumare to save us as they pursued us across the sand and suddenly the sand turned into black venomous ants and began to attack the snakes. The snakes tried to bite them, but as they tried to do this they began to bite themselves and every one of the snakes began to kill themselves and poison themselves and the poison began to affect them and by doing this they succeeded in killing themselves off. We took this opportunity to return to the palace. We found the place where Ojola was lying in state. He had been placed upon a huge platform. We looked inside his intestines and found two calabashes. One was gold and one was silver; when I turned the top the gold fell out to the ground, gold coins fell out. Enia opened the silver calabash and silver fell out. He became rich.

Everyone ate well in the palace and drank some liquor

and some of us had too much to drink and began to dance the Hi Life. When it became evening we packed up our belongings and carried them on the top of our heads, and the smaller ones among us took care of some. We had more than we had when left the home of Baba. We walked over the dead snakes and headed toward the highway for home.

We followed Ijam's lead. Ijam presented a song based upon his name. We would say Ijamba and he would say Foriti. As he lifted his feet one at a time, we would lift our feet and clap our hands. And so on. Thus we left the City of Snakes, a place where Ojola-ibinu was the King.

ACKNOWLEDGMENTS

Conjure, Chattanooga, A Secretary to the Spirits, and *Points of View* include poems previously published as *New and Collected Poems* by Ishmael Reed, Atheneum, 1988, and in the Poems section of *The Reed Reader* by Ishmael Reed, Basic Books, a member of the Perseus Book Group, 2000, pp. 327–422.

Many of these poems were previously published in three collections by Ishmael Reed: *Conjure, Chattanooga,* and *A Secretary to the Spirits.* Many of these poems have appeared in journals and anthologies, and acknowledgment is gratefully made to the editors of *The Berkeley Fiction Review, River Styx, California Living, The Buffalo Evening News, Up Late: American Poetry since 1970, Wind Row, New Letters, Lips, The Berkeley Poetry Review, Black World, Mark in Time, Yardbird Reader, Umbra, Black World, Liberator, Essence, Ikon, Scholastic, For Now, In a Time of Revolution, Where's Vietnam?, Poets of Today, The Poetry of the Negro 1745–1970, The New Black Poetry, Soulscript, The L.A. Free Press, The Black Poets, Dices,* and *The Norton Anthology of Poetry.*

Some of the material in this book, set to music by leading jazz composers, can be heard on two albums, *Conjure I* (American Clave, 1985) and *Conjure II* (American Clave, 1988), produced by Kip Hanrahan and rereleased by Pangaea and Rounder Records (1995), which are available in LP, cassette, and compact disc, as well as the forthcoming *Conjure III,* also produced by Kip Hanrahan, on the Blue Note label, recorded in a 2005 studio session.

Gethsemane Park libretto © Ishmael Reed 1994, 1995, 1996, 1997, 1998, 2000

Poems appearing in the section *New Verse* first appeared in print, frequently in earlier drafts, in the following list of publications:

"Paper-Weight" in *The Berkeley Poetry Review*, No. 23/24, Spring, 1990, p.14.

"Four Untitled," in *The Berkeley Poetry Review*, Issue 26, 1992–93, p. 38.

"Azabu Kissaten de," *The Subaru Monthly*, January, 2004.

"America United," in *Peace News*, published and edited by John Bryan, Issue Number Two, 2001, p. 16 and *September 11, 2001, American Writers Respond,* edited by William Heyen. Silver Springs, MD: Etruscan Press, 2002, pp. 322–328.

"El Paso Monologue," in *A Gathering of the Tribes,* Volume 4, Number 1, 1994, Steve Cannon, editor-in-chief, p. 18.

"I am not the walrus," in *Long Shot,* Volume 18, Hoboken NJ: Long Shot Productions, Nancy Mercado, editor, 1996, pp. 177 and 178

"I am not the walrus" and "El Paso Monologue," in *Spirit & Flame, an anthology of Contemporary African American Poetry* edited by Keith Gilyard. Syracuse NY: Syracuse University Press, 1997, pp. 176–77 and 177–78.

"Memphis," in *River City, A Journal of Contemporary Culture,* Volume 18, Number 2 and Volume 19, Number 1, Special Double Issue, Summer, 1998, pp. 163–164.

"Let Oakland Be a City of Civility," in *The Oakland Tribune,* January 5, 1999, p. 9 and *The San Francisco Examiner,* January 5, 1999.

"Senior Citizens," in *Five Fingers Review 18,* General editor, Jaime Robles. Berkeley, CA· Five Fingers Press, 1999, pp. 17–19.

"A Bank Branch Closes," in *Drumvoices Revue, Special 10th Anniversary Anthology of Poetry, Fiction & Drama,* founding editor, Eugene B, Redmond. Spring-Summer-Fall, 2003, Volume 11, Numbers 1 & 2, p. 225.

"Ohun Pataki," in *Drumvoices Revue, A Confluence of Literary, Cultural & Vision Arts. Fall/Winter 1992/93, Vol. 2, Nos. 1 & 2,* founding editor, Eugene B. Redmond, p. 75.

"Guys," in *Re/Mapping the Occident* edited by Bryan Joachim Malessa and John Jason Mitchell, pp. 133–134.

"He Picked A Fight With Haitians," in *Long Shot,* Volume 23, Hoboken NJ: Long Shot Productions, Nancy Mercado, editor-in-chief, 2000, p. 183.

"I Want to Be a Right Wing Family Values Type of Man," *The Argonaut,* Volume XXIV, Whole Number 4529, December, 2003, Warren Hinckle, editor and publisher, p. 22.

"When I Die I Will Go to Jazz" (as "Ted Joans Said 'Jazz Is My Religion' "), in *Shuffle Boil,* Issue No. 4, Summer/Fall 2003, edited by David Meltzer & Steve Dickison, pp. 2–3.

"Tennessee's Revenge," in *The San Diego Reader.*

"Hands On," in *Long Shot,* Volume 27, Hoboken, NJ, p. 186.

"Going East" is one of 126 poems included in the Berkeley Poetry Walk, designated a National Poetry Landmark by the Academy of American Poets. The poems are set in cast-iron tiles with porcelain enamel lettering and installed in the pavement of Addison Street in the downtown Arts District of Berkeley, California, as part of a public arts project conceived by landscape architect John Roberts and curated by poet Robert Haas. The poems in the Berkeley Poetry Walk have also been anthologized in *The Addison Street Anthology, Berkeley's Poetry Walk*, edited by Robert Hass and Jessica Fisher (Berkeley, CA: Heyday Books, 2004), p. 164.

"Inspiration Point, Berkeley" appeared in *The New Yorker*, Aug. 29, 2005, p. 48.

"Snake War" is based upon chapter VIII of Yoruba author D. O. Fagunwa's *Igbo Olodumare* (The Forest of God), "Ojola-Ibinu Ti Ise Olori Ejo Aiye Gbogbo," or "Ojola-Ibinu, the King of Snakes everywhere."

ISHMAEL REED is author of six books of poetry, one opera libretto in verse, six plays, and nine novels, and is the editor of numerous anthologies and magazines. His poetry collaborations with musicians have resulted in three CD collections: *Conjure I: Music for the Texts of Ishmael Reed* and *Conjure II: Cab Calloway Stands in for the Moon,* originally from American Clavé and most recently reissued by Rounder Records, and the forthcoming *Conjure III* from Blue Note. A poem written in Seattle in 1969, "Beware: Do Not Read This Poem," has been cited by Gale Research Company as one of the approximately 20 poems that teachers and librarians have identified as the most frequently studied in literature courses.